The Unshakable **Truth** That ~~Changes~~ ~~Everything~~

# GOD
## IS FOR
# YOU

*DavBlunt Ro 8:31*

## DAVID **BLUNT**

*God Is For You*
© 2024 by David Blunt

Published by Insight International Inc.
contact@freshword.com
www.freshword.com
918-493-1718

All rights reserved. No part of this book may be reproduced or transmitted in any form or by any means, electronic or mechanical, including photocopying and recording, or by an information storage and retrieval system, without permission in writing from the author.

Unless otherwise noted, all Scripture quotations are taken from the New King James Version®. Copyright © 1982 by Thomas Nelson. Used by permission. All rights reserved.

Scripture quotations marked (NLT) are taken from the Holy Bible, New Living Translation, copyright ©1996, 2004, 2015 by Tyndale House Foundation. Used by permission of Tyndale House Publishers, Carol Stream, Illinois 60188. All rights reserved.

Scripture quotations marked (KJV) are taken from the King James Version of the Bible, public domain.

Scripture quotations marked (MSG) are taken from The Message, Copyright © 1993, 2002, 2018 by Eugene H. Peterson.

Scripture quotations marked (AMPC) are taken from the Amplified® Bible (AMPC), Copyright © 1954, 1958, 1962, 1964, 1965, 1987 by The Lockman Foundation Used by permission. lockman.org.

Scripture quotations marked (AMP) are taken from the Amplified® Bible, Copyright © 2015 by The Lockman Foundation. Used by permission. lockman.org.

Scripture quotations marked (NIV) are taken from the Holy Bible, New International Version®, NIV®. Copyright © 1973, 1978, 1984, 2011 by Biblica, Inc.™ Used by permission of Zondervan. All rights reserved worldwide. www.zondervan.com. The "NIV" and "New International Version" are trademarks registered in the United States Patent and Trademark Office by Biblica, Inc.™

Scripture quotations marked (YLT) are taken from the 1898 YOUNG'S LITERAL TRANSLATION OF THE HOLY BIBLE by J. N. Young, (Author of the Young's Analytical Concordance), public domain.

ISBN: 978-1-960452-01-6
E-Book ISBN: 978-1-960452-02-3
Library of Congress Control Number: 2023914797
Printed in the United States of America.

# Endorsements

God is for you! The way we think about God greatly affects the way we live and relate to Him. In *God Is For You*, my friend David Blunt challenges us to reconsider our view of God, proving that these four words "God is for you" are more than a positive thought or a theological concept—they're a beacon of hope in the midst of fear, uncertainty, and chaos.

>John Bevere
>Best-Selling Author and Minister
>Cofounder of Messenger International and MessengerX

In a day of a superabundance of frightening, weird, and negative news, my friend David Blunt has created a holistic prescription of godly good news that encourages, corrects, and edifies us to be better than ever! It is a clear message full of light for a dark world.

>Bishop Dale C. Bronner
>DMin, Founder and Senior Pastor of Word of Faith Cathedral
>Atlanta, Georgia

What a wonderful title, *God Is For You*, and what a wonderful, encouraging, and life-changing book that Pastor Blunt has written to show us that we have a "good" God and He really is for us! All of us have had trauma in our lives and we did the same thing Pastor Blunt did; we asked, "Why, God?" This book will give you open doors to live the life that God promised, a life of abundance in spite of all the things that the world throws at us. You will understand that our God can and will do everything He promised, but we must allow Him to do it His way, in His time, and in His wisdom! A marvelous book to share with new believers and also longtime believers. It will be a life-changing experience as you apply these truths that God has given us to know that He is for us and always has been and always will be.

>Dr. Marilyn Hickey
>Marilyn Hickey Ministries

A *treasure* for your life; a *tool* you can share. You don't have to be stuck in a self-sabotaging mindset that limits your ability to actually *see* and *understand* just how much God *unconditionally* LOVES YOU and is *unequivocally* FOR YOU!

Why? Because Pastor David Blunt's book, *God Is For You*, uncovers a treasure trove of priceless, proven (Bible-based) principles that can show you how to *transform* self-defeating behaviors and *overcome* any shame-based agonies from past mistakes (and traumas) . . . with a fresh infusion of faith that you'll receive as you read and apply the life-building truths he freely shares from his heart with you (based on his years of personal experiences).

You'll enjoy and discover how Pastor Blunt's stories are like the rumble strips on the road that make you suddenly aware that you may have drifted from your lane in life. You'll find yourself being graciously guided back to clearly see God's proper perspective of YOU . . . and just how much He wants you to experience an ample, abundant, fulfilled life with Him.

I'd recommend that you get more than just one copy because *God Is For You* can also make an ideal gift for family and friends who may be struggling with doubt, disappointment, dissatisfaction, failure, frustration, or feelings of being forgotten, and loneliness. It's an inspirational tool that graciously imparts a clear-cut reminder that God not only *loves* them, but He is *for* them *here* and *now* in their *present* (regardless of their past) and in their *future* (regardless of their current circumstances).

    Paul Landry
    International Ministry and Media Development Consultant
    Seattle, Washington

Pastor Blunt is one of my favorite pastors who reminds us that God is bigger than our problems. His book, *God Is For You*, does just that. A great book that was proven to work before it was written.

    Richard Montanez
    Author, philanthropist, and creator of the worlds #1 snack
    Flamin' Hot Cheetos
    Former VP of PepsiCo and movie producer

I was captivated as I read the pages of David Blunt's book, *God Is For You*.

All my growing-up years, my father, Oral Roberts, poured into me and much of the world that God is a good God . . . that He was for me, and not against me . . . that He had a plan for my life . . . and it was a good plan!

Now, David has brought this great truth to the forefront again. And it's the right timing, especially when you look at the world today and witness how the cancel culture society is trying to close the book on God and box Him out of our lives.

This book will build your faith to believe better than you have ever believed before.

As you read this book, you will feel the mighty presence of a God who loves you and desires to be at the very center of your life because He is a good God.

Enjoy, and I know you will.

        Richard Roberts
        B.A., M.A., D. Min.
        Chairman and CEO of Richard Roberts Ministries

If you want an extraordinary book with insights to propel you into your extraordinary future, *God Is For You* is that kind of book. From non-Christian to mature Christian, let Pastor David Blunt reveal to you what took him from God-cynic to God-lover and how that changed the trajectory of his life. You will be inspired to believe the simple truth that God's plan for you is good, even better than you've realized to this point, and nothing, not failure nor the past, is greater than God's power to dictate that future.

David's heart for the success of others comes through in each chapter, and he shares so many simple yet powerful truths. This book can lead you into life, significance, and fulfillment. Fall in love with God for the first time—or all over again. God is for you.

        Dr. Jerry Savelle
        Jerry Savelle Ministries
        Founding Pastor of Heritage of Faith Christian Center
        Crowley, Texas

I absolutely love the way Pastor David Blunt gives the reader an undeniable insight into how God believes in us, wants the best for us, and is cheering us on into our destiny. This book will change your perspective of God and help you discover that no matter what you might be facing, God is on your side and will help you each step of the way. God is for you!

  April Osteen Simons
  Hope Coach

This book is a must-read. Pastors David and Kim have over forty years of ministry proof that indeed God is for us. My wife, Tracy, and I and many others have not just witnessed it but as a result of his revelation we have experienced it! Let's Go!

  Aeneas Williams
  NFL Pro Football Hall of Fame Inductee
  Pastor of The Spirit Church, St. Louis, Missouri

# Dedication

I would like to dedicate this book to my wonderful wife, Kim; our two sons, Daniel and Stephen; our daughter-in-law, Tamara; and our three grandchildren, Ava, Ethan, and Lana.

# Contents

Foreword ........................................................................................ 11
Acknowledgments ........................................................................ 13
Introduction: God Wants You to Let Him Change
                Your Life for the Better ........................................ 15

1. **God** Is For **You** ..................................................................... 19

2. **God** Is **Good** ........................................................................ 31
   He Understands You

3. **God** Is **Good** ........................................................................ 39
   The Blessing of God Is in His Presence

4. **God** Is **Good** ........................................................................ 49
   Let Him Take You to a New Level

5. **Your** Future Is **Good** ........................................................... 61
   More Exceptional than You Can Imagine

6. **Your** Future Is **Good** ........................................................... 71
   Discover God's Will for Your Life

7. **Your** Future Is **Good** ........................................................... 81
   Walk into the Future God Has for You,
   One Step at a Time

8. **Your** Future Is **Good** ........................................................... 91
   Keep Following the Green Lights

9. **Your** Future Is **Good** ......................................................... 103
   Flourish

10. **Your** Future Is **Good** ....................................................... 113
    When Your Faith Is in God

11 **Your** Future Is **Good** ..........................................................................127
   Favor, Family, Friends, and Opportunities

12 **God** Is for **Your** Security.....................................................................139
   Finances

13 **God** Is for **Your** Security.....................................................................149
   Focus on Him

14 **God** Is for **Your** Security.....................................................................159
   Safety

A Final Word of Encouragement:
Let God Show You that He Is for You .......................................................171

# FOREWORD

I have been privileged to be friends with David and Kim Blunt, senior pastors of Church on the Rock, for over thirty years. To know them is to see this message walked out—*God is for you*.

They live it, believe it, and teach it. Thousands have been impacted by this message, including me. Pastor Blunt always gives me the feeling that he is for me, and God is too. His deep relationship with the God who is for us affects everyone he is in contact with.

I've encouraged Pastor Blunt to write this book for almost as long as I've known him. It's his life message. I believe God gave him this word for you right now.

It's certainly one of the most amazing facts—almost unbelievable to the human mind—that the creator of the universe, our heavenly Father, is for us. This book reveals the many ways God is for you. You will be profoundly encouraged by how deeply almighty God is on your side—He is in your corner. You're on His mind right now. He is not neutral or apathetic about you. He is not your problem or your enemy. His goodness pursues you, and every day He offers you new mercy.

I think once we get to heaven, we'll all realize how much God was for us here on earth. The good news is, you can know and live in that revelation now. Receive His goodness, mercy, and perfect love.

The heart of the gospel is that God is for you. So, I encourage you to open up to this most important truth as you read this book. You will be forever changed.

> John Mason
> Author of *An Enemy Called Average* and numerous other best-selling books

# ACKNOWLEDGMENTS

I would like to thank my dear friend, John Mason, for all of his help, insight, and encouragement to finally write this book. I would also like to express my gratitude to Daniel, Margaret, Michal, Linda, and Michelle for their research, creativity, and hard work in helping this dream become a reality.

# INTRODUCTION
## GOD WANTS YOU TO LET HIM CHANGE YOUR LIFE FOR THE BETTER

Many people have a wrong perspective of God. They don't know that He wants to do good things in their lives.

God wants to guide you into good things. He may lead you by the Holy Spirit. He may lead you through godly people. He wants to give you divine associations, appointments, and assignments to help and show you step-by-step how to fulfill the purpose He has for your life, a good purpose. He wants to give you favor and open doors for you in order to take you places you wouldn't be able to go on your own. He wants to heal you. He wants to protect you. He wants you to succeed. He wants to move on your behalf.

People have a wrong perspective of God because they have false beliefs. They have false beliefs because of different experiences they've had, or a particular situation they've been in, or from learning them from somebody else with erroneous beliefs. Some denominations teach false beliefs! Other denominations teach "God is for you," but the teaching does not reflect the knowledge of how much He is for you.

For God to do the good things He wants to do in your life, you need to have the right perspective of Him. You need to form the right picture of Him. You need to find out for yourself who God really is. You need to find out that He is a good God, that He is for you, and that He has a good plan for your life. You do this by going to the Bible, the Word, and finding out what He is like and what He tells you He has for you. The Word is the basis above all else for guiding you. It encourages you and builds your faith to live a life so good, you would have thought it was impossible.

As early as first grade, I had a heart for God and went to church by myself, even after my family had quit going at that time. I grew up in a denominational church and believed many things about God that were false. Then as an adult, I had a void in my life. I tried to fill it with things I wanted. And I did—I had everything I ever wanted. But I was hungry for more. I was hungry for change. I knew there was something God wanted me to do, but I was running from it because I had a wrong picture of Him.

When I was in a bookstore one day, I found a teaching that showed me there is another perspective of God from the one I had grown up believing. From that point, I began to find out what the Word says about God being for me. I found out who God is and what He wants to do in our lives today, tomorrow, and the day after that. I learned that I needed to get a right picture of God. So I began to change my perspective.

The way to change your false beliefs about God is by learning the truth in His Word and applying it. As you hear the Word and do what it says, your perspective begins to change. The Word says that "faith comes by hearing, and hearing by the Word of God" (Rom. 10:17). The Word encourages you and builds your faith. As you build your beliefs on hearing and learning the truth of God's Word, you realize that you can trust God to do what the Word says He will do. Trust is another word for faith. You can trust Him.

# INTRODUCTION

You can have faith in Him. Your perspective will change to the belief that all things are possible for you.

Sometimes things happen we don't understand, bad things—delay, disappointment, derailment, difficulty. Depression and discouragement can follow. Or we prayed for something, and it didn't happen, something we thought should happen. If we know who God is from the Bible, we can trust Him even though bad things have occurred because we know He won't abandon us—we know He will never leave us nor forsake us. (Heb. 13:5.) We know ". . . If God is for us, who can ever be against us?" (Rom. 8:31 NLT). We learn that God can cause all things to work together for the good. (Rom. 8:28.)

God wants you to let Him show you how to live a more purposeful, meaningful, happy life. But we have to work with God, not against God. There is always a partnership. We are co-laborers, co-workers, with Him. (1 Cor. 3:9.) When I was running from God, I couldn't receive all He wanted to pour into my life, all the good He desired to give me, because I wasn't doing my part. So we have our part, and God has His part.

In many miracles described in the Bible, we see that people had their part, and God had His part. One example is in 2 Kings 5. Naaman, the commander of the army of the king of Aram, was healed of leprosy after he followed the instructions of Elisha, the prophet of Israel, to wash in the river Jordan seven times. At first, after Elisha sent the instructions by way of a messenger, Naaman was angry that Elisha had not come out and prayed for him directly. So Namaan started to leave, but his servants convinced him to follow the instructions. And because Naaman did His part according to God's directions, he was healed. So Naaman had his part, and God had His part. (2 Kings 5:1-14.)

Because I was one of those people who had everything I needed and wanted but was dissatisfied with life, I know what it's like to think, *Is this all there is—isn't there more to life than this?* The answer is, "Yes, there is more." If this describes you, there is meaning and purpose available for you. There is meaning, purpose, and happiness available for you beyond any you could have imagined.

There are people who have everything they want and people who are hurting and hopeless. There are people who already know that God is for them, but they don't have any idea how much. No matter what state those people are in, they are hungry for more. They know there's something good out there for them, but they don't know what it is or how to reach it.

For nearly forty years I have been teaching people who God is and the good He has for them, and I have seen people's lives change dramatically for the better. In the church my wife and I started, Church on the Rock, there have been tens of thousands of people who have come to know God's goodness through the Word. Thousands have learned how to be co-laborers with God. Many now live their lives so well that they would have thought it impossible. And they are reaching others with the message of what Jesus did for us and how to receive what He has done for them.

No matter where you are or what you've done, you can experience God's goodness starting today. So, as you read this book, open yourself to all your heavenly Father has for you. Almighty God, the creator of the universe, is for you!

# 1

# **GOD** IS FOR **YOU**

God has life-changing blessings for us that will affect the way we live today, tomorrow, and the next day. God wants to satisfy our lives with good things. But when you hear these things, maybe you think they don't apply to you. Maybe you believe that God isn't for you.

In fact, you may be someone who sees the title "God Is For You" and thinks, *Every time I've turned to God, it didn't work. He's never been for me my whole life! So, I feel like He's actually against me.*

You may be someone who thinks, *God is for you? That's the opposite of what I've seen and heard.* But then you pause and think, *However, maybe it's worth looking into.* And when you start reading the book, you find out that God is nothing like what you thought, or had been taught, or had heard. You find out how to experience for yourself the truth of what "God is for you" means in your life.

In my own experience, I moved away from being aware of God's caring nature and attending church by myself as a young child. My family had gone to church together. We used to go every time the doors were open. I had a great heritage. My dad was a deacon. My mom was a Sunday school teacher. But when my parents walked away from God and church, that was the time I kept going by myself. I got myself up on Sunday morning and went to Sunday school by myself and came home all by myself. I had my own Bible, a little kid's Bible, that I kept by my dresser.

My family moved to another town. It was a great town, like Mayberry on "The Andy Griffith Show" TV series that ran for years. The pastor came to our house and invited us to church. My parents were ready for a transition, and we all went and started attending church together again! That's when I gave my heart to the Lord. It was a wonderful church with great people, and we were always taught that God loved us. But we never heard "God is for you." Instead, we heard about all the things we weren't supposed to do.

So then I grew up in the church. But something happened that resulted in me wrestling with thoughts about whether I wanted to serve a God who would not answer my family's prayers about my brother Rick.

Rick was six years older, and Rick was my hero. He died unexpectedly from a blow to the head that activated a brain tumor. Although the church prayed and fasted for his life, my brother still died. Rick hadn't accepted Christ along with the rest of my family, but in the hospital, our pastor led Rick to Christ. Rick is with the Lord, but our prayers didn't save his life.

Rick had served in Navy Intelligence in Morocco. He was married, had an awesome wife, and had his whole life ahead of him. He looked like a hero. Rick was 6 foot 4 and weighed about 250-260. He liked cars, and I liked cars. He enjoyed motorcycles, and I enjoyed motorcycles. Everything Rick did, I wanted to do. Then he had one of those freak accidents. He was cleaning his fireplace in the basement of his house, started to rise up, and hit his head on a pipe. When he died within the week, my world shattered.

Even though it was wonderful in many ways, my church was one of those churches that tries to explain what they find unexplainable with the mindset of responses like this: It isn't God's will to heal everybody; God puts sickness on us to teach and train us.

When all of this happened, I was a teenager. I was a junior in high school. I began to struggle with the thoughts, *I don't know if I want to serve this kind of God who would take my brother—who would kill my brother—and not answer prayer.*

After I went through the grieving, the anger process, and even bitterness, I began searching for myself to find out, "Just what kind of a God is this?"

God started giving me little inclinations about His true nature, how good He is, and that He is for us and wants to work on our behalf. Then, He started leading me to the answers to my questions.

Somebody gave me a Bible with footnotes that started showing me there was a different perspective of God from the one I had. God brought me little things like that to begin showing and teaching me how good He actually is. If you know God, you know how He works like that.

Through the Holy Spirit, He started bringing things like another book, or something else I would see or hear. And then a minister came to our church and preached a positive message that God is a good God. I had never heard anybody preach like that!

I had a glimpse of that message before. My grandmother received the Lord through Oral Roberts's ministry. Oral Roberts's overriding message was, "God is a good God." Then in this beginning of God moving toward me in a greater way, seeking me out by providing me with these little insights, the minister came to our church and taught that positive message in a series that I sensed in my spirit was true. It resonated in my spirit, and I started finding out for myself God is for me; He wants me to have an abundantly good life; He has a future planned for me full of blessings and favor, and He wants to work on my behalf.

Although I had a wonderful, solid, strong family, I hung around with the wrong people in grade school, junior high, and high school. People told me, "You'll never make it. You'll never amount to anything. You're going

## GOD IS FOR YOU

to wind up in prison. You're going to be dead before you're thirty." I ran around with those friends who were a bad influence because I felt accepted by them and rejected by other people.

When I was fourteen years old, I stole a bicycle. It didn't take long for my little Mayberry town police to find and arrest me. I had to go to court. My parents loved me dearly, but they were frustrated with me. They told the judge, "We can't do anything with Dave. We've tried. We don't know what to do with him."

The pastor of our church, Leroy Butts, was in the courtroom. He stood up and said, "Judge, can I say something?" And the judge said, "Yes." He said, "I'm his pastor, and I know he's made mistakes, but I believe in him. I believe he's a good boy." The judge agreed to give me another chance with a warning! "Okay. I'm going to put him on probation for a year based on what you said about him."

Because my pastor stood up for me, he kept me from going to reform school. Although I had to make weekly visits to the court for a year, I was saved from going down a different path that could have led to potentially devastating consequences. That path probably would not have led me to where I am and what I understand about God today.

*Sometimes it's just a simple remark or a word of encouragement that can change your life's direction.*

This was another glimpse of the message "God is a good God." There was my pastor. There was a person God put into my life, who said, "I'm for you," to represent God to me in my life.

Sometimes God will use a person to say, "Hey, I'm for him." He doesn't use an audible voice from above, but He will use a person to literally say, "I believe in you. I support you. I'm not going to abandon you. I'm going to stick through the course with

## GOD IS FOR YOU

you." This is one of the many ways God works to show us how much He loves us and wants to work in our lives.

Another person God brought into my life was Charlie "Tremendous" Jones, bestselling author, and renowned speaker. Sometimes it's just a simple remark or a word of encouragement that can change your life's direction.

He came to our church. We had him there for a sweetheart banquet. He said, "You will be the same person in five years as you are today except for the people you meet and the books you read."

I had been all through high school without reading a book, but that night when he said that, it stuck. Those words jolted me.

When my wife, Kim, and I attended the banquet, we had been married for two years. Kim and I had been fighting and fussing, quarreling. We loved each other, but we couldn't stand each other. I was unhappy. I had no purpose or meaning in life. So I tried to get everything I could to satisfy that void.

I had a good job in management. I had a wonderful, beautiful wife. I had a brand-new Corvette and a motorcycle. We bought land in the country and were going to build a house. I had everything I wanted. But I was in that place where nothing could bring me happiness. God gave me another glimpse of His goodness through the teaching I found in the bookstore that I found to be so instrumental.

I knew there was something God wanted me to do, but I had been running from it. And that's when I said, "God, I don't know what you want me to do, but I surrender. I surrender my life to you. There's got to be more to life than this. I've got to have meaning in my life. But whatever I do for you, I don't want to be average. I just don't want to be average!"

After this experience of surrendering to God, I wanted to change my life dramatically. I needed to go to college. So Kim and I went to college, and all through college, I was an A student on the honor roll.

Ultimately, God used those words by Charlie "Tremendous" Jones to change the direction of my life. Moreover, Charlie became a mentor to me, encouraging me and, later, mentoring my son Daniel for many years.

I had been running from God because I didn't know He wanted the best for me. I grew up thinking that God's approval of me was based on what I did. I believed if I made mistakes or didn't completely follow His commandments in the Bible, He would not be on my side. I believed He supposedly did all sorts of bad things to teach and correct people. It was like God was up there with a club waiting for me to do something wrong. All these were wrong views of God. I don't think that I would have followed God if I had stayed with that picture I had of Him.

## CORE BELIEFS ARE VERY IMPORTANT TO YOUR VICTORIOUS CHRISTIAN LIFE

A few years ago, I learned something very important about the strength that comes from working out and doing exercises for your core. When I was speaking on a Wednesday night, I leaned over, and something in my body snapped. I was in a great deal of pain for the rest of that service and after it. I couldn't lift anything. I couldn't lift my grandkids. I couldn't lift a suitcase. I was in such pain that I couldn't tolerate it. So I finally went to the doctor. The doctor said it was a hernia and I needed an operation. So the surgeon operated and put a net in there.

After the operation, I had just as much pain for days, weeks, and months. I still couldn't lift my grandkids. I still couldn't lift a suitcase. I was in so much pain in my daily duties of life I didn't know what to do.

My doctor, who focuses on nutrition and wellness, and is our nutritionist, was speaking at our church. He said, "Pastor, what you have to do to get rid of this pain and get back on track is start doing core exercises." He told me that the strength of your core determines how strong the rest of your body is. He gave me a few exercises for building the core.

So I began to do those exercises, and I began to get stronger. And the pain began to lessen! So I went to a gym and started on a program I've been doing for three years, working out five days a week. My trainer tells me the exercises he has me do regularly are for my core.

*Our core beliefs determine the strength of our walk with God.*

Just as we build our strength physically by doing exercises for our core, we build ourselves spiritually by focusing on four core Christian beliefs. Our core beliefs determine the strength of our walk with God. Kim and I practiced these core beliefs while raising our children, and our children apply these same core beliefs with our grandchildren.

Hosea 4:6 (KJV) tells us, "My people are destroyed for lack of knowledge."

I encourage you to pray as I do every day for God to show me if I have any wrong believing in my life because I want to replace it with the truth. If our beliefs are false, then we move in the wrong direction, as we've seen.

**The first core belief: God has a plan for your life.**

"And we know that God causes everything to work together for the good of those who love God and are called according to His purpose for them" (Rom. 8:28 NLT).

We may not understand what is going on in our life right now. We may have a tendency to question. "Has God forgotten me?" "Is God angry with me?" "Has God left me?" "Has He forsaken me?" "Does God not love me?" Even though those feelings and thoughts keep coming up, we must remind ourselves daily and never forget, "God has a plan for my life."

Just because we are Christians doesn't mean we are immune from bad things happening. But it puts us in line for God to turn the bad into good for us. As a Christian, you need to know that God is working behind the scenes, although you may not see Him or feel Him, although you go through times when you don't understand what's happening.

It is important to recognize that this Scripture verse tells us that God turns bad into good for those who love him and are aligned according to his will. Unfortunately, this verse in Romans is often misquoted to mean that "God causes everything to work together for good . . ." leaving out the rest of the verse, for ". . . those who love God and are called according to His purpose for them." This promise is clear that it is only for those who love Him and are committed to His plans for them.

**The second core belief: God is for you.**

"If God is for us, who can be against us?" (Rom. 8:31).

God wants to give you favor. He can take you to levels you would never have imagined because of His favor. Of course, things may not turn out the way you would expect. But when you love Him and are called according to His purpose, during those times, you know you can understand that God is still moving on your behalf in ways you can't see.

**The third core belief: God loves you.**

"And I am convinced that nothing can ever separate us from God's love. Neither death nor life, neither angels nor demons, neither our fears for today nor our worries about tomorrow—not even the powers of hell can separate us from God's love" (Rom. 8:38 NLT).

Romans 8:38 means don't let any battle you're involved in allow you to question God's love for you.

God's love for us shows He is for us.

**The fourth core belief: God has made you more than a conqueror.**

Overwhelming victory is ours when "we are more than conquerors through him that loved us" (Rom. 8:37 KJV).

Can anything ever separate us from Christ's love? Does it mean he no longer loves us if we have trouble or calamity, or are persecuted, or hungry, or destitute, or in danger, or threatened with death? (As the Scriptures say, "For your sake we are killed every day; we are being slaughtered like sheep.") No, despite all these things, overwhelming victory is ours through Christ, who loved us. (Rom. 8:35-37 NLT)

## BELIEVE THAT GOD LOVES YOU

In today's times, we need to know God and understand the good He has for us. He wants us to succeed; He wants us to affect others for Him despite the circumstances.

The most important belief you can build, which is the basis for knowing God is for you, is that He loves you.

We have an enemy, the devil, and the Bible refers to him as "the accuser of our brethren" (Rev. 12:10 KJV). The devil ". . . is a liar and the father of lies" (John 8:44 NLT).

When we ask God for something and it doesn't happen, the devil comes throwing accusations, throwing lies at us, wanting us to buy into them. He gives us thoughts like, *God does not love you; He has not forgiven you.* He tells us in our minds: *You're a nobody. You're ignorant. You're a failure. You're broke. Nobody likes you.*

All those nicknames, all those names you were called on the playground growing up, were assigned to defeat, distract, and humiliate you to keep you from achieving God's plan for your life. Everything that's weakened you—ridicule, criticism, all kinds of accusations, making fun of you—was sent your way by the devil through a means that many times people had no idea about. The devil does this to try to get you to lose your confidence, doubt God's love for you, and forfeit your destiny.

When Kim and I decided to go to college, we went to see the pastor of our church who married us. I explained our intentions to sell the house, my motorcycle, and everything else to go into the ministry. The pastor looked at me and said, "Dave, you'll never make it. You don't have what it takes to be in the ministry."

This was like my experience in grade school, junior high, and high school when people told me, "You'll never make it; you'll never amount to anything." This time I knew the truth behind what was happening. I knew God was for us and wanted us to go into the ministry.

What if I had listened to that pastor and not gone into the ministry? Today our church is large, and we are reaching thousands of people with the message that God is for them. We have three campuses. There are people all over the world who consider our online campus their church.

Evander Holyfield, the four-time world champion professional boxer, occasionally visited our church. One time I asked, "Evander, what gives you that mental toughness when you enter the ring?"

He answered, "Pastor, what gives me my mental toughness is my daily confessions, such as declaring, 'God is for me' when I enter the ring."

We are all facing some form of a ring or battle today. From learning how much God is for us, we will be able to enter the ring with confidence to win rather than with the expectation of defeat in the battles of life.

If we listen to the devil's accusations long enough, we begin to believe the lies. We will say, "God, do You really love me? If You really love me, then why aren't I healed? If You really love me, then why don't I have a job? If you really love me, why is the answer taking so long?"

"God, I don't understand what's going on. I thought I was supposed to have an abundant life." "I prayed, and I'm still sick." "I lost my house. I don't understand that!" "Have you forgotten me?" "Are you angry with me?" "Don't you care?" "Where are you?"

When people ask questions about God, such as, "Why did He do that?" "Why did He let that happen?" "Why did my prayer go unanswered?" "How could I possibly think that everything that has happened could mean that God is for me?", I understand because I've lived it. And as a pastor, I've heard every challenge and question that most people will face. I've heard it all.

All of us have had imperfect lives. But I have learned, and I believe it with all my heart, that God is for me. Even when I've felt like a total mess, He's still for me. Even when I've made all sorts of mistakes, He's still for me. Romans 11:29 tells us, "The gifts and calling of God are without repentance" (KJV), "irrevocable" (NKJV).

No matter how much we have messed up or how long we have done nothing, there is still something God wants us to do. If I let Him, God will guide us back into fulfilling our purpose.

A first step toward understanding how much God loves you and how much He is for you is not accepting the devil's accusations that God doesn't love you. When the devil accuses you with a lie, as 2 Corinthians 10:5 says, we bring a thought into captivity by speaking God's Word and promises, replacing the wrong thought with the truth, and begin living a life of overwhelming victory!

*No matter how much we have messed up or how long we have done nothing, there is still something God wants us to do.*

# 2

# GOD IS GOOD

## HE UNDERSTANDS YOU

We can tell what someone is really like by looking at the person's attributes. If you want to know God and how good He is, study his attributes. This is what David in the Bible did to grow closer to God. He had the right perspective of God.

David's life is an example for us. In his life we see how to live our lives every day trusting that God is for us. And as a result of the way David lived, we see God moving in a mighty way to bring David overwhelming victory.

In my research, all the commentaries, all the historians, and all the theologians agree that David's Psalm 139 is the greatest Psalm of all of the Psalms in showing us how to experience and grow closer to God. In this Psalm, David looks at three attributes of God. God has many, many more attributes, but David focused on three. David studied them and thought about them throughout the day—he meditated on them. He applied what he learned. He took action in his daily life based on who he knew God to be from meditating on the attributes. And the Psalms and other Scripture verses are filled with examples of David overcoming his enemies as a result of his close relationship with God.

David was a king. He was a warrior, and he was a worshipper. David was strong in faith and moved in the Lord's strength to victory!

David overcame Goliath, a champion out of the camp of the Philistines, who King Saul and the army of Israel were afraid of, so much so that all the men of Israel fled! David felled Goliath with one stone from his sling, then killed him. Before that, David killed a lion and a bear to rescue a lamb one of them had taken from his father's flock. David took the lamb out of the mouth of the one who held it, catching him by his beard and killing him! (1 Sam. 17:4, 11, 24, 34-36, 48-51.)

Despite being a young shepherd boy, David was able to convince King Saul to allow him to face Goliath on behalf of Israel. "David said moreover, The Lord that delivered me out of the paw of the lion, and out of the paw of the bear, he will deliver me out of the hand of this Philistine..." (v. 37).

*If you want to experience a deeper relationship with God, if you want to see Him move in a mighty way for you as He did for David, and if you're going to overcome your enemies, just mimic what David did.*

In the Psalms, David specifically described who the Lord was to him. The Lord was David's strength. He was David's protection. He saved him from his enemies. (Ps. 18:1-3 NLT.)

David spoke of the Lord's "wondrous works" and His "marvelous kindness" (Ps. 145:5; Ps. 31:21 KJV). David said, "Oh, how great is Your goodness" and ". . . All the Lord's promises prove true . . ." (Ps. 31:19 NKJV; Ps. 18:30 NLT).

David loved God. He already had a close relationship with Him and wanted an even more intimate relationship with Him. And, as we see in Psalm 139, David had enemies to overcome because of the circumstances he faced. He experienced depression, discouragement, fear, worry, anxiety, and doubt. He faced the same kinds of enemies we face.

If you want to experience a deeper relationship with God, if you want to see Him move in a mighty way for you as He did for David, and if you're going to overcome your enemies, just mimic what David did.

This is the key, the secret, right up front, for how to have a deeper relationship with God. If someone had a cure for cancer, people would want to know what it was right away. If someone had a cure for migraine headaches, people would want to know what it was right away. If someone had the cure for any disease, people would want to know what it was right away. Well, this is the cure for getting closer to God and experiencing His goodness. It's what we see David doing in Psalm 139. So let's look at the first of God's three attributes, or characteristics, that David studied.

## GOD UNDERSTANDS

Have you ever felt misunderstood? Sometimes I felt it a lot. Down through the years, people have misunderstood me. How about you? They misunderstood something you said or something you did. Or somebody thought they knew you when they really didn't know you. And you go through life thinking, *I wish somebody would just understand me.*

Well, God understands you. God knows the inward us, the hurts history, the hang-ups. God knows the inward you, and God knows the outward you. God knows every moment of your life. He knows every movement; He knows every motive, and He knows every maneuver. God knows everything about you. God is all knowing. He is omniscient.

Omniscience is the first of three attributes of God that King David studied, which he wrote about in Psalm 139. It is described in verses 1-6. Verse 1 says, "O Lord, You have searched me and known me." God has searched us and knows us. He knows everything about us.

## GOD IS FOR YOU

God knows the enemies you're facing. He knows if you're hurt today or if you're hung up on something today. He knows if you feel alone. He knows if you're going through frustration, anxiety, or have questions. God knows everything. And yet, with all He knows about us, He still loves us. He is still for us. He still cares about us. He still believes in us.

Many people look at God being omniscient, being all knowing, as a negative. They think, *Oh, God's watching over me to find something wrong with me.* But, no, that is not what this chapter is about. God is watching over you because he knows *the possibilities.*

Yes, God knows the past, all your past, even if it's bad. God knows your present; He knows if it's challenging. The all-knowing God knows why you are the way you are. He knows the history that made you who you are today—the good and the bad. He knows you through and through. And this also means He knows all your potential and possibilities. When others put you down, remember that God knows your potential and your possibilities. When David asked what would be done for the man who killed Goliath and took away the reproach of Israel, his oldest brother, Eliab, ridiculed him. (1 Sam. 17:26-28.) But David knew his potential in God. He proceeded on, and he was the one who defeated Goliath!

Psalm 139:5 tells us, "You go before me and follow me. You place your hand of blessing on my head" (NLT). God knows who you can become. He knows a perfect plan to take you into your future. He knows your future; He knows if you're uncertain. He wants you to know not to worry. He has you covered. He knows where you're going. God will go before you to orchestrate your future. He wants you to let Him lead you. He wants you to allow the One who created you to direct your life.

And He follows you. He goes behind you. He will turn all your mistakes, all your messes, into miracles for the future. He will turn all your hurts into healing. Where you fell short and where you were disappointed, He will turn those things around. He is in your past, and He is in your future.

He knows where you've been, He knows what you're going through. He knows where you're going, and He knows the best way to get there. Many times you won't know how He's going to take you there, when He's going to do it, or who He is going to do it through. Verse 6 says, "Such knowledge is too wonderful for me; it is high, I cannot attain unto it" (KJV).

> He knows where you're going, and He knows the best way to get there.

Many times we can't figure out or reason out how God is going to do something. He knows and has a plan for the best way to meet our needs. His plan will meet our needs and provide for us in a way beyond our imagination. We can't bring God down to our level of thinking. To fulfill His plan, we need to let Him guide us.

Don't let your circumstances shrink what you think God can do. Don't let your past, the fear of the future, or uncertainty shrink what you believe God can do. And don't let well-meaning but misguided people or feeling disappointment shrink what you think God can do.

You don't know your full potential. You don't know your full possibilities. That is one reason to learn to trust God and concentrate on doing your part so that He will be able to do His part and take you into a future beyond anything you could have planned.

Once Kim and our family went to Israel with Hilton Sutton. He was a Bible teacher, author, and one of the foremost authorities on Bible prophecy. We were in the Upper Room. He came over, hugged me, and whispered in my ear, "Dave, I just wish you'd begin to see yourself as God sees you, and the plan that He has for your life and your future."

That event impacted my life. I've never forgotten it. Again in my life, God used a person to say He is for me—this time, in a greater way than I had previously thought. He impacted me through a friend to show me how much He is for my future.

## KNOW GOD

The most important thing there is, according to the Bible, is that we understand and know God personally. This means practically, directly discerning and recognizing His character and attributes.

*The important thing about a person is what that person thinks about God.*

Jeremiah 9:23 tells us (my paraphrase), let not the people who are wise glory and boast in their wisdom, degrees, and skill; let not the people who are fit glory and boast in their strength and their power; let not the people who are wealthy glory and boast in their houses, vacations, earthly wealth, and physical gratification. Instead, Jeremiah 9:24 tells us:

> But let him who glories glory in this,
> That he understands and knows Me. . . .

And (NLT):

> . . . who demonstrates unfailing love and who brings justice and righteousness to the earth, and that I delight in these things. . . .

Glory in this: that you understand and you know the God who knows you.

A. W. Tozer said, "What comes into our minds when we think about God is the most important thing about us."

The important thing about a person is what that person thinks about God. Our picture of God determines what perspective we have of Him, as we have seen. Our view of God also determines how we see ourselves and how we see other people. So if we have a wrong picture of God, we have a false picture of ourselves and an inaccurate picture of other people in our lives. Our relationship with God determines our outlook, and our outlook determines our outcome. Our outlook is our outcome.

When I surrendered to God, I told Him I didn't want to be average.

## GOD IS GOOD | HE UNDERSTANDS YOU

On our dates when we were in college, Kim and I used to walk down to the Dairy Queen on Sunday afternoons, get ice cream, and dream about our future. We drew a picture of the inside of the sanctuary of the church we were dreaming about. This was in 1977. It looked like the sanctuary of our building today! I said at that time, back in college, "I see a church of five thousand people." It wasn't going to be average. Today we have six thousand active members! We knew not to limit God in our expectations or shrink what we thought He could do. And we learned how to let Him take us into our future. Our outlook was our outcome.

How we see God can determine the decisions we make and the direction we take. When we have the right perspective of God, we see our circumstances of today as He sees them. Then, through studying and meditating on God's attributes and acting on what we have learned, like David, we will see that ". . . All the Lord's promises prove true."

But first, to fully experience how much God is for you, the fullness of His goodness, and all He has for you, you must understand who He is and take the step to accept Him into your life.

In order to know God and grow in your relationship with Him, you must form a relationship with Him. God knows you inside and out and loves you. He has compassion for you and wants to work in you and on your behalf in a mighty way.

If you do not have a relationship with God, do you want one with that kind of God? Jesus provided the way to form a relationship with God. Jesus died on the cross to take our sins on Himself to give us forgiveness so that we can have a relationship with the holy God who has no sin and be with Him forever. Your sins are forgiven when you receive Jesus.

To receive Jesus and form a relationship with God, pray this:

Heavenly Father, I repent of my sins. I believe Jesus Christ is the Son of God. I believe He died on the cross for me and took my sins on Himself so that I am forgiven. He took my sins—past, present, and future—and they are forgiven! Jesus died, was buried, and rose again to make the way for my sins to be forgiven and for me to have eternal life with You. Jesus, come into my heart; come into my life. I receive you now as my Lord and my Savior. Fill me with the Holy Spirit. Use my life to make a difference, in Jesus's name!

Now God can work to change you from the inside out and transform your life into something wonderful or greater than it was before!

It isn't what we hear that changes our lives; it's what we hear, think about, and apply that changes our lives. Coming to church and hearing the teaching won't change us. Thinking about what was taught and using it changes us. As we meditate and take action, we build a solid foundation of understanding God is for us and living in the results of that revelation.

Matthew 7:24-25:

Therefore whoever hears these sayings of Mine, and does them, I will liken him to a wise man who built his house on the rock: and the rain descended, the floods came, and the winds blew and beat on that house; and it did not fall, for it was founded on the rock.

To change our outlook and our outcome, we both hear and do the Word.

Begin meditating on this first of the three attributes of God in Psalm 139 that we will look at in the following chapters. Meditate on Psalm 139:1-6 verses on the omniscient, all-knowing God. Think about how He will go behind you to turn your mistakes around into good things for the future. Think about how He will go before you to orchestrate an exceptional future in a way you couldn't imagine. Use these verses with other Scripture verses on God's goodness to replace the lies of the accuser, the devil. And through this, continue to grow closer to God to experience all He has for you.

The Lord wants to show us His goodness, as He did to David, and He wants to show it in practical ways. He wants to prove to us His promises are true. We need to learn how to let Him.

# 3

# GOD IS GOOD

## THE BLESSING OF GOD IS IN HIS PRESENCE

God is ever present. When you know how to be aware of His presence, when you know how to relate and connect with Him, you make Him bigger than your problems.

He is with you all day and all night. When you get up in the morning, He is with you. He knows what you need to succeed in every area that day to conquer the giants, the Goliaths, and He will guide you. He is with you in your daily routine. He is with you on your path all day.

He is with you at work. He is with you in the doctor's office, the courtroom, and the lawyer's office. He is with your child and you in the principal's office. He is with you taking your kids to soccer, softball, or camp. He is with you at home—in the bedroom, the kitchen, the back porch, and the front porch. He is with you when you sit in a chair and when you stand up. He is with you when you sleep. He's here, there, and everywhere. He never leaves you. (Heb. 13:5.)

# GOD IS FOR YOU

King David meditated on three of God's attributes to grow closer to God, which he wrote about in Psalm 139. And as a result of David's close relationship with God, we learn through the many examples in the Psalms and other Scripture verses that David overcame all his enemies. We saw that the first attribute is omniscience—God is all knowing. The second attribute is omnipresence, described in verses 7-12. Omnipresence means God is always present with us.

What does that mean? It means you're never alone. If you're a person who struggles with feeling lonely, a revelation of the omnipresence of God is the cure for loneliness. There is the sweet companionship of the Lord through the Word and the Holy Spirit. The Lord comforts you. He gives you peace. But we also need quality relationships with people. He will guide you into circumstances and meaningful connections with people. He holds you up. He supports you. God rules over the nations (Ps. 22:28), yet he wants an individual personal relationship with you.

## ENJOYING GOD

The presence of God is where the blessing of God is.

Some people don't like the idea of God being ever present. Some people are afraid of God. Some people don't understand the blessings God's presence brings. Because many people have wrong beliefs about God and church, they don't want anything to do with Christianity.

There are many people who aren't interested in becoming Christians because they think there are things they will need to give up. They think they will need to give up having fun. They hear about legalistic rules that some denominations or other churches teach dictating what Christians are and aren't supposed to do. Or they hear other false beliefs that are taught. Most of those rules, and the false beliefs, are based on tradition and have no basis in the Word. They do not present the true picture of what having a relationship with the God who is for them is like.

# GOD IS GOOD | THE BLESSING OF GOD IS IN HIS PRESENCE

What will people who become Christians really need to give up? Things like hangovers. Living an eternity in hell, which they don't know about or refuse to believe. We need to tell them the truth. We need to tell them about who God is and what a relationship with Him, and our lives, are really like when we follow Him. A life of following God is filled with great benefits when we know how to let God show us He is for us in the specific ways the Word explains.

*A life of following God is filled with great benefits when we know how to let God show us He is for us in the specific ways the Word explains.*

## GOD'S BENEFITS

David tells us the Lord "daily loads us with benefits" (Ps. 68:19). That means today. That means these benefits are available now. Psalm 103:2-5 tells us what some of those benefits are. He forgives all our sins, He heals all our diseases. (NLT.) He redeems us from death (NLT), from destruction (NKJV), from the pit (AMP). He crowns us with love, lovingkindness, and tender mercies. (NLT, NKJV.)

He fills our lives with good things, our youth is renewed like the eagle's. (NLT.) God is not against us having things, just as long as things don't have us. Just as long as the things aren't more important to us than He is and we start living for them instead of for Him. People need to know God is for them. He is for them being successful in their careers and their callings. He is alive, relating with us and moving for our good.

There are more benefits of living with an awareness of God's presence. They are practical to help us in our daily living.

**He shows us the path of life. (Ps. 16:11a.)**

Many people today are confused, frustrated, have no direction, no vision, no goal, and no dream. They've given up on all of that. But this verse tells us He will show us the direction for our lives.

Where in God's presence is the place of blessing? It is mainly in the place of His direction. There is no confusion there because "God is not the author of confusion, but of peace . . ." (1 Cor. 14:33 KJV).

*What God wants is for us to want to have a greater experience with Him.*

The omnipresent God wants to show us direction for our lives just as we saw in looking at the first attribute David wrote about in Psalm 139, omniscience. The ever-present and all-knowing God wants to direct our steps to take us into the future He has for us and keep us aware of His presence, the place of blessing.

Jeremiah 10:23 tells us our lives are not our own. (NLT.) It is not in our limited ability, compared to God's ability, to direct our own steps or plan our own course. (AMP, KJV, NLT.) No matter how successful we are, we don't know enough, we don't have enough—we don't have the resources, the portfolio, the net worth, or the network—to direct our own lives and take us to the level God desires for us.

What God wants is for us to want to have a greater experience with Him. And through this, He wants us to allow Him to direct our steps to a future greater than we could have imagined.

**God wants us to have joy. (Ps. 16:11b.)**

In Psalm 16:11 David tells us, ". . . In Your presence is fullness of joy; at your right hand are pleasures forevermore." There are pleasures, plural, more than one. A major benefit of being in the presence of God is fullness of joy. With all the negativity in the world today, it looks as though many of us need a shot of joy. The devil wants to steal our joy. He wants to ruffle our feathers.

The devil wants us to become offended, upset, and walk in unforgiveness. He comes to steal, kill, and destroy (John 10:10), and he wants to steal our joy. But God wants us to enjoy Him and our Christianity. We need to learn how to enjoy Him! Victory is in God's presence. It's the place of blessing. It's a place of joy.

**God wants us to have peace. (John 14:27.)**

Many people look for peace in the wrong places. Where is the right place to find it? In a church with Bible-based teaching. In small groups and fellowship. Through reading and meditating on the Word. Jesus said, "Peace I leave with you . . ." (John 14:27 KJV).

**God will defeat all our enemies. (Ps. 9:3.)**

Some of us have enemies of fear, worry, anxiety, unforgiveness, panic, insomnia, prejudices, sickness, disease, and fear of failure. Some people think they can't handle life anymore. They feel like giving up.

Psalm 9:3 tells us, "When my enemies turn back, they shall fall and perish at Your presence." We're to be world overcomers. (1 John 5:4-5.) And I relate to what people experience with facing some of those enemies. I couldn't do what I need to do from the time I get up in the morning until I go to bed without intentionally being in God's presence. Keeping my focus on Him defeats the enemies trying to steal my joy and stop what I'm obeying Him to do.

Depression is a major enemy. It is prevalent. Many people hurting with it come to church. The omnipresent God knows what we're feeling. Isaiah 61:3 says there is ". . . beauty for ashes, the oil of joy for mourning, the garment of praise for the spirit of heaviness . . ." (KJV). I call that transformation the greatest change.

Isaiah 60:1: "Arise [from spiritual depression to a new life], shine [be radiant with the glory and brilliance of the Lord]; for your light has come, and the glory and brilliance of the Lord has risen upon you" (AMP).

The glory of the Lord is the presence of God. It is possible to rise to a new life from the depression in which circumstances have kept you. God wants to help you fulfill the purpose He has for you by directing you and guiding you step-by-step. He wants you to let Him lead you into a future with more meaning and with happiness, one that is more fulfilling than you could have dreamed possible.

## RECEIVING GOD'S BENEFITS

There are many people who don't want to become Christians because they think the message of "God is for you" isn't for them. They think the things they've done are too terrible for God to forgive. They think God couldn't possibly be for them. If you are one of the people who thinks this way, it is not true!

No matter how terrible the things you've done are, God loves you. He loves you so much that He sent Jesus, His Son, to die on the cross for your sins. The Bible says that whoever believes in Him will not perish but will have everlasting life. (John 3:16.) "Whoever" includes everyone. It includes you. Believe in Jesus and you will have everlasting life with Him and God the Father in heaven and the opportunity to let Him show you how much He is for you in your life on earth.

God is not empty religion. He is not about a set of rules to follow in order to be good enough to go to heaven. Deciding to receive the free gift of what Jesus did for you (Rom. 6:23 NLT) is the way to become a Christian and begin living the life God has for you now.

## GOD IS BIGGER THAN YOUR PROBLEMS

People who are Christians, Christ followers, still experience challenges. We have adversity in our lives just like people who haven't accepted Christ.

The Bible says it rains on the just and the unjust. (Matt. 5:45.) What does that mean? It means we all go through trouble, tests, and trials. We all deal with pressure, stress, and the cares of this life. But there's a difference for those of us who are Christ followers. We have Someone working in us and for us who can help us through everything we experience so that we will come out better on the other side. With Him, we can experience overwhelming victory!

Your outlook determines your outcome, and your uplook at God determines your outlook. Your uplook is your outlook, and your outlook is your outcome.

*How big is your God that you're looking at today?*

How big is your God that you're looking at today?

My load is too heavy to try to carry it without God. Being a husband for almost a half century, a father, a grandparent, an employer, an entrepreneur with a multimillion-dollar corporation, staying up in a down world—I couldn't do it all without looking at a big God. No way.

My uplook at God is at a big God who does big things. And He does do big things. When Kim and I went to the Dairy Queen and dreamed about our future, our uplook was big. We saw a big church of five thousand people. And because the outcome God had was that and even bigger, we have been able to minister to thousands and thousands of people.

## GOD CONSCIOUS

God's presence is the place of blessing. You and I want to know how to practice His presence every day and focus on being God conscious. As Psalm 139 tells us, He is always present. We can't flee from His presence. His hand is always there to lead us. His right hand holds us. We don't know what the future holds, but we know who holds our future. Even in the darkness, we are not hidden from Him. (vv. 7, 10-12.) We can walk in darkness and not be afraid. We can go through the darkest season of our lives and know He is present to guide and help us.

He is there through that season of divorce, through that season of cancer, and through that season of loss of a loved one. He is there through the loss of a job, the loss of all retirement funds, and through the aftereffects of the COVID-19 pandemic and the cultural events of today. He is there as the cure for loneliness. He is there in the darkest days of our lives. The night shines as day to Him. The darkness and light are the same to him. (v. 12.)

If you don't feel His presence anymore, He is not the One who moved. You did! He is always present. We want to learn how to recognize Him and how to become very aware of His presence.

How do we enter into the presence of God? There's surrender. When you know God is for you and working on your behalf, it makes sense to surrender to what He wants to do in your life. Follow the guidance He gives you. Follow Him step-by-step.

The presence of God is where the blessing is, and the presence of God is where the power of God is. Luke 5:17 describes a day when Jesus was teaching "and the power of the Lord was present to heal . . ." (KJV). Jesus healed the man with palsy whose friends let him down through the roof because of the crowd, but the scribes and the Pharisees were unaffected. They were critical. (vv. 18-21.) They were not open to entering in.

To enter into the presence of God, there's obedience. Obedience brings the presence of God into manifestation.

Worship will take you into God's presence. At the beginning of our services at Church on the Rock, we spend twenty minutes in praise and worship. The Bible says to enter into His presence through praise. Sing! "Serve the Lord with gladness: come before his presence with singing" (Ps. 100:2 KJV).

Reading the Word will take you into His presence. This is one reason why meditating on His attributes, as David did, is so important. Meditating on who God is will take you into His presence. Gratitude will take you into and keep you in His presence—being thankful and grateful in your present circumstances for what you have.

## GOD IS PRESENT AROUND US AND IN US

God is not only ever present around us; He is in us. In John 14:2 we read that Jesus explained to His disciples that He was going to His Father's house to prepare a place for them. (He was going away because He was going to be crucified.) Jesus said the Father would give them another Comforter, who would abide with them forever. (v. 16.) The Comforter would be with them and in them. The Comforter is the Spirit of truth, the Holy Spirit. (v. 17 KJV, NLT.) Jesus said, "When I am raised to life again, you will know that I am in my Father, and you are in me, and I am in you" (v. 20 NLT). When we receive Jesus, God's presence is in us!

The world, those who haven't received Jesus, cannot receive the Holy Spirit. (v. 17.) They don't know how much they need Him. The Holy Spirit brings supernatural comfort. This is not the comfort people get from illegal drugs or alcohol or other addictive methods to find comfort. People who receive Jesus will receive the Holy Spirit as the Comforter.

In Old Testament times, the Holy Spirit was the presence of God on earth and dwelled in the temple, the Tabernacle. Only the high priest could enter into the presence of God, and only at a certain time. The Holy Spirit dwelled with the people, but only in the sense that He dwelled in the Tabernacle. Sometimes He came upon them to do extraordinary feats. But He was never within them.

In the New Testament, the new covenant, through Jesus's death, burial, and resurrection, Jesus provided the way for the Holy Spirit to live in us when we receive Jesus. We, our bodies, are the temple of the living God. (2 Cor. 6:16.) "As God has said: 'I will dwell in them and walk among them . . .'" (v. 16). That is powerful. ". . . greater is he that is in you, than he that is in the world" (1 John 4:4 KJV).

## HINDRANCES TO ENJOYING GOD'S PRESENCE

To experience the fullness of God's presence He intends, what you and I want to do is remove anything in our lives that would hinder us from entering in.

There may be habits, too much attention paid to social media, the news overwhelming us with the world's view and hopelessness, relationships that are taking us in the wrong direction, or thoughts and attitudes we haven't taken into captivity that alienate us from experiencing the presence of God. We may be letting false beliefs stand in the way of us surrendering and obeying Him.

We can hinder entering into God's presence through words we speak. Ephesians 4:29-30 tells us not to allow corrupt communication to come out of our mouths and not to grieve the Holy Spirit. If we quarrel and fight and live in strife, we can't expect to feel the presence of God in our house. We learn in Job 22:28 that we can declare a thing, and it will be established for us, and the light will shine on our ways. I want the peace of God in my house. What we say is important.

## ENJOY LIVING IN GOD'S PRESENCE

The benefits David wrote about are available for you today—forgiveness, healing, redemption from death and destruction, and God's love, lovingkindness, and mercy moving in your life. He wants to guide you every moment and wants your enemies—fear, anxiety, and others—to be defeated. He wants you to experience the joy of being in His presence and His peace.

Practice His presence every day. Stay aware of Him. Relate to Him and let Him move through you. Receive what the God who is for you has for you. He wants to daily load you with benefits.

# 4

# GOD IS GOOD

## LET HIM TAKE YOU TO A NEW LEVEL

Smith Wigglesworth said, "The power of God will take you out of your own plans and put you into the plan of God." That's exactly where we all want to be.

David wrote that God's thoughts about him were so precious they could not be numbered. (Ps. 139:17 NLT.) God feels the same way about us. The all-powerful God who wants to move in a mighty way for us regards us as precious. David began his description of God's third attribute he wrote about in Psalm 139 by praising the all-powerful God who wonderfully made him. (v. 14 KJV.) The third attribute is omnipotence, meaning God is all-powerful. We read David's description of this characteristic in verses 13-18.

### FULFILLING YOUR PURPOSE

Another Scripture verse that refers to being wonderfully made is Ephesians 2:10: "For we are God's masterpiece . . ." (NLT). God created the heaven and everything in it—the sun, the moon, the stars, and the planets. And He created the earth and everything on it—the plants, the animals, and man. Yet, out of all of His creation, He considers mankind, you, His greatest creation. You are God's masterpiece above anything else He created.

Ephesians 2:10 goes on to describe the purpose God has for us: ". . . He has created us anew in Christ Jesus, so we can do the good things he planned for us long ago" (NLT).

In order to fulfill the purpose God has for us, we must be created anew in Christ Jesus. God wants us to find our place and purpose and experience who we are in Christ. He wants us to follow the steps He directs us to take into the great future He has for us. And He wants to lead us into doing the good things He planned for us long ago. But He won't be able to do these things unless we are newly created in Christ.

*You were deliberately, specifically, lovingly, placed and positioned here for your purpose in this time, such a time as this.*

Being newly created in Christ means becoming a new creation. "Therefore, if anyone is in Christ, he is a new creation; old things have passed away; behold, all things have become new" (2 Cor. 5:17). This is what happens when you accept Jesus into your life—you become a new creation.

The frustration that comes with feeling as though you have no purpose ends when you form a relationship with God through Jesus and follow the guidance of the Holy Spirit within you step-by-step. "For in him we live, and move, and have our being . . ." (Acts 17:28 KJV).

You were deliberately, specifically, lovingly, placed and positioned here for your purpose in this time, such a time as this. The book of Esther shows us an example of someone God had placed in a particular time for a particular purpose. God put Esther in the position of a queen to save her people, the Jews, from death in the many provinces the king ruled, from India to Ethiopia. (Est. 1:1 KJV.) Esther's uncle, Mordecai, said to her, ". . . Who knows if perhaps you were made queen for just such a time as this?" (Est. 4:14 NLT).

If you think you would rather have lived in a different time, no. This is the time God saw as the best for you and me to live. But, He has a specific purpose for us to be here. And that purpose benefits others. "When you realize God's purpose for your life isn't just about you, He will use you in a mighty way," says Dr. Tony Evans.

We read in Psalm 139:13 the details David wrote about being a wonderful creation: "For You formed my inward parts; You covered me in my mother's womb." Then he wrote, "I will praise You, for I am fearfully and wonderfully made; marvelous are Your works, and that my soul knows very well" (v. 14).

David said that his soul knew very well that he was fearfully and wonderfully made, and that God's works are marvelous. Our soul needs to know that very well. When we meditate on Scripture verses such as these and on who the all-powerful God is who created us, we are transforming our mind, will, and emotions to think and believe in line with who the Word tells us God is. This is called the renewing of our mind, being ". . . transformed by the renewing of your mind . . ." (Rom. 12:2 KJV). This is also called the law of replacement.

"Don't copy the behavior and customs of this world, but let God transform you into a new person by changing the way you think. Then you will learn to know God's will for you, which is good and pleasing and perfect" (Rom. 12:2 NLT). This again points to meditating on who God is. We should stop comparing ourselves with others and stop listening to the negative things the world has to say and demonstrate to us, and instead, replace those things with what the Word says.

See yourself as God sees you. Instead of letting the accuser tell you lies to get you to put yourself down, what should you do? Praise God, for you are fearfully and wonderfully made. Believe you are extraordinary because God says you are.

## A NEW LEVEL

David wrote about God's power being displayed in the marvelous work of creating him. And David wrote about his many experiences of seeing the all-powerful God move in a mighty way on his behalf.

God rescued David from powerful enemies who were too strong for him; He led him to a place of safety because He delighted in David. (Ps. 18:17-19 NLT.) With God's strength, David could crush an army. (v. 29 NLT.)

David said God's help had made him great. (v. 35 NLT.) David chased and caught his enemies, not stopping until they were conquered. (v. 37 NLT.) The Lord armed David with strength for battle. (v. 39 NLT.) He gave David victory over his accusers and appointed him ruler over nations. (v. 43 NLT.)

The all-powerful God gave David not only victory, but overwhelming victory. David was operating on a new level.

David said:

...people I don't even know now serve me.
As soon as they hear of me, they submit; foreign nations cringe before me.
They all lose their courage and come trembling from their strongholds.
(Ps. 18:43-45 NLT)

We saw that David began his description of God's third attribute by praising the all-powerful God for fearfully and wonderfully making him. When he moved into writing about the ability of the omnipotent God to overcome his enemies, he wrote about everything that was against him.

David wrote about everyone and all the circumstances that were against him, and he wrote about God's power to move on his behalf.

Beginning with Psalm 139:19, we see that David knew in advance that God could powerfully overcome his enemies. This comes from David's knowledge of the good God who was for him because of his relationship with Him.

Psalm 139:19-20:

Oh, that You would slay the wicked, O God!
Depart from me, therefore, you bloodthirsty men.
For they speak against You wickedly;
Your enemies take Your name in vain.

Verse 21 states: "Do I not hate them, O Lord, who hate You? . . ." That's an interesting statement.

Verse 21 continues: ". . . And do I not loathe those who rise up against You?"

Verse 22: "I hate them with perfect hatred; I count them my enemies."

David is saying, "If they're Your enemy, God, they're my enemy."

*If something is an enemy of God's, it should be our enemy.*

If something is an enemy of God's, it should be our enemy. So, although David faced enemies who were people, let's not think of the enemy as people in these verses. Instead, let's think of the enemy as fear.

Anxiety is fear. God doesn't want us to worry, fret, be upset, uptight, or unhappy. If God hates something, we should hate it. We should count it as our enemy. Emotional enemies we face are God's enemies. Fear is an enemy. We should hate it when fear tries to rule our lives to stop us from experiencing what God has for us! We have the tool to use to overcome it. We know how to renew our minds to God's goodness toward us instead of focusing on and accepting enemies like fear. And we will trust that the all-powerful God will move on our behalf to rescue us and lead us to a place of safety and victory. Trust God's plan because He knows best.

## VICTOR MENTALITY

What David wrote next shows us that he refused to be a victim. David knew God and knew God would lead him to victory. David knew God was bigger than all his enemies, no matter how big they looked. (Ps. 139:19-22.)

If David had allowed himself to have a victim mentality, he would have kept focusing on his enemies. He could have kept focusing on the bloodthirsty men who were against him. He could have kept focusing on the circumstances, pressure, the people, the struggle, and the hard times. He could have blamed other people for what was happening to him. He could have stayed right there in a position to be defeated by his enemies. But he didn't. Instead, he turned his attention to God in prayer because he didn't want to be a victim.

Some people with a victim mentality blame others or God for their situations. Instead, they need to follow God into success by growing up and being mature. They need to look at themselves and ask God to change them and concentrate on what He wants them to do to move forward. If they are not open to receiving correction or direction from God, it is likely they won't fulfill their potential.

We need to have the same perspective as David, or we will live as victims, defeated. We need to keep focusing on God as bigger than all our enemies. "For with God nothing shall be impossible" (Luke 1:37 KJV). God is bigger than your mistakes, your despair, your pain, your anger, your doubt, your shame, your fear, your past, your hate, and your mistakes. Say to your challenge, "God is bigger than you."

David was determined to be a victor. He had the right perspective in his life of who God is, who he was in God, and the good God had for him. He had the correct view of the call upon his life. So later in Psalm 139, we read that David asked God to search him, change him, and lead him to continue molding him into who he was to become.

## YIELDING TO GOD'S GOODNESS

> Search me, O God, and know my heart;
> Try me, and know my anxieties;
> And see if there is any wicked way in me,
> And lead me in the way everlasting. (Ps. 139:23-24)

Verse 23 in the *King James Version* says, ". . . try me, and know my thoughts."

David opened his heart to correction and direction from God and yielded to it. These tools allow God to work in our lives in a way that guides us into experiencing all the good He has planned for us.

Author and speaker Lee Cockerell, a former executive with Walt Disney World, invited me to attend a webinar. Immediately after the webinar, I received an email from him asking for feedback. He led a team of forty thousand Cast Members and developed Disney Great Leader Strategies to train and develop the seven thousand leaders at Walt Disney World, and he was asking me for feedback![1] Winners are learners. Winners want feedback, and they will adjust, adapt, and correct.

David said, "Search me, O God, and know my heart." We could say that David wanted feedback!

God knows your habits and your routines. He knows all your thoughts—your perceptions. So let Him show you habits, attitudes, or other areas in your life you need to change that might be holding you back from moving into where you want to be and where He wants you to be. He knows how

---

[1] "Biography," https://www.leecockerell.com/about. "Implementing the Disney Great Leader Strategies," September 12, 2017, https://www.leecockerell.com/disney-leadership-strategies.

to help you change. He knows the resources and relationships you need to connect more closely with Him.

> *Every day I surrender, I yield, and I give my life totally to God.*

Ask Him to try you and search you. Let Him lead you and guide you into what you need to change. Tell Him, "You know my weaknesses and my strengths, and I need your help." Turning to Him helps you stop trying to fix everything yourself.

Ask Him, "Is there a wrong attitude in me? Do I have a wicked way or a wrong thought? Do I have wrong mindsets toward people? Your ways are higher than our ways, and Your thoughts are higher than our thoughts, according to Isaiah 55:9. If there's anything in my life that is wrong, search me, show me, change me, and lead me in the way that's everlasting. Show me how to change."

Every day I surrender, I yield, and I give my life totally to God. I give him my marriage, my career, my employees, my vendors, my health, and I give him my future and my destiny. I give him my mistakes and my victories. I say, "Oh God, search me; I'm open for feedback." "Someday you will be really grateful that God gave you what you needed instead of what you thought you wanted" (Stephanie May Wilson).

## ALL ENEMIES OVERCOME

Many Psalms reveal the enemies David faced because of his circumstances that are similar to the ones we face. In Psalm 6:6, we see one example. Although he was strong, David said, "I am weary with my groaning; all the night make I my bed to swim; I water my couch with my tears" (KJV). This was part of David's reaction to the enemies he was facing. Psalm 6:7 continues, "My eye wastes away because of grief; it grows old because of all my enemies."

Many Psalms, in addition to Psalm 139, show us that David knew he would overcome those enemies through his relationship with God because he knew God was for him. David said, "I would have lost heart, unless I had believed that I would see the goodness of the Lord in the land of the living" (Ps. 27:13). We see that because of his relationship with God, David knew God would move for him and that God did move for him: "I waited patiently for the Lord; and he inclined unto me, and heard my cry. He brought me up also out of an horrible pit, out of the miry clay, and set my feet upon a rock, and established my goings" (Ps. 40:1-2 KJV). And we see David's confidence in the Lord to deliver him later in Psalm 6:

> ...the Lord has heard the voice of my weeping.
> The Lord has heard my supplication;
> The Lord will receive my prayer.
> Let all my enemies be ashamed and greatly troubled;
> Let them turn back and be ashamed suddenly. (vv. 8-10)

The all-powerful God accomplished extraordinary physical feats through David. We may not be in a position of needing to crush a whole army or of defeating a champion who represents victory over an entire people as David did! Normally in our daily lives, we do not face the types of physical challenges and enemies like the ones David did. But we all have challenges today. At times we have significant physical challenges to overcome, and like David, we have enemies to conquer that we deal with as a result of circumstances. All your great victories will begin with a battle. But we know that the all-powerful God will overcome the enemies we face for us and through us when we know Him, and we trust in who He is.

## WORDS OF AGREEMENT WITH WHO GOD IS

When meditating on God's attributes, we saw that David studied them, thought about them, and took action based on them. But much of David's meditation involved singing about them. For example, in the songs of praise, the Psalms that David wrote, he sang about the omniscient, all-knowing God who went behind and before and blessed him. (Psalm 139:5 KJV, NLT.) He sang about the omnipresent, ever-present God who was always there to guide him and support him with His strength, even in the worst situations. (vv. 8, 10-12 NLT, KJV.) And he sang about the omnipotent, all-powerful God who wonderfully made him with marvelous workmanship and gave him victory over his enemies. (vv. 14, 19 KJV, NLT.)

When David sang, he was speaking words in agreement with who He knew God to be.

Psalm 19:14 tells us:

> Let the words of my mouth and the meditation of my heart
> Be acceptable in Your sight,
> O Lord, my strength and my Redeemer.

If God monitors our thoughts and words, they must be important. And our thoughts and our words are acceptable only if they're in agreement with God's Word. So when the words we speak agree with God's Word, we call this positive confession.

## WORDS AND DIRECTION

Words have a lot to do with determining the direction of our lives. James 3:3-5 tells us that our tongue is like a bit in a horse's mouth and the rudder of a ship.

*Words have a lot to do with determining the direction of our lives.*

After Kim and I graduated from college, we did an internship, but we didn't know where we would go at the summer's end. We didn't have a church to go to where we would serve. I kept telling Kim that by the end of summer, we would have a place to go and a church to serve in. So all summer long, I kept saying aloud, "We're going to know where we're going by the end of summer."

We knew from Job 22:28 that we can declare a thing, and it will be established for us, and the light will shine on our ways. So I kept speaking aloud, declaring we would have a place to go by the end of the summer.

At the end of the summer, the night before we were to leave, we had packed everything up in our Gran Torino Ford car. But we still had no place to go.

Then the phone rang. A pastor called me and said, "Hey, I heard you're looking for a place to serve. Are you going to drive by our church? Stop and do an interview."

We drove there and interviewed. And we got the job! God is never late, but He's right on time. Faith in God includes faith in His timing. All summer, I had declared aloud that we would have a place to serve in a church by the end of the summer, and we watched God establish that declaration.

## TRANSFORMATION

God wants us to know His character. Understanding His character through meditating on His three attributes David wrote about in Psalm 139 and other Scripture verses will change our thoughts to think in line with who He is. And knowing God's character will change us and allow Him to direct us in great detail.

*Jesus is more powerful than the devil, and Jesus lives in us.*

We all are in a spiritual fight. Jesus is more powerful than the devil, and Jesus lives in us. Meditating on who the all-knowing, ever-present, and all-powerful God is, instead of the lies the accuser tells us, keeps us open to allowing all the good God wants to do in our lives. Meditating on God's attributes gives us a revelation of how much God is for us and demonstrates how much He wants to work for good for us in specific ways.

## GOD IS FOR YOU

When David meditated on these three attributes, everything turned around for him. Meditating on God's attributes will turn things around in your life, as well.

What is it that God wants to change in your life? What do you want to change in your life? What specifically does this mean? What do you need to say about it based on who God is and what His Word says?

Transformation happened for David. And transformation, life change, will happen for you and me. Meditating on God's attributes took David to a new level with God. He can do the same for you. God is omniscient, omnipresent, and omnipotent. He's all knowing, always present, and all powerful. So rejoice in who God is and how He is for you!

# 5

# YOUR FUTURE IS GOOD

## More Exceptional than You Can Imagine

God wants us to win in life. Not just once in a while, not just at church. God wants us to win every day, all the time, and in the future.

God tells us about the good future He has for us. The words He gave to Jeremiah for the Israelites in Babylonian captivity are also for us today: "'For I know the plans I have for you,' declares the Lord, 'plans to prosper you and not to harm you, plans to give you hope and a future'" (Jer. 29:11 NIV).

Psalm 138:8 says, "The Lord will work out his plans for my life . . ." (NLT), "The Lord will perfect that which concerns me . . ." (NKJV). And the Lord, ". . . is able to do exceedingly abundantly above all that we ask or think, according to the power that works in us" (Eph. 3:20). God works through our asking and our thinking. He works through our meditation on who He is and His attributes, and He works through us speaking words in agreement with who we know the God who is for us is.

Because God has a future for us beyond our imagination, we need to stop every day and look at the size of God: big God, big future. Then, once we're living in that future, we look back and realize God was already working in our present to orchestrate it, although we may not have been aware of why things were happening at the time. God is already in the future working on our behalf through events He is arranging in our present. He is already in the future working for our good. "He isn't asking you to figure everything out. He's asking you to trust that He already has" (Anonymous).

*Move boldly forward and trust the next chapter—when you know the author.*

## WHEN YOU HAVE A GOOD FUTURE, YOU WON'T WANT TO GO BACK

When you know you have a promising future ahead of you, you will live motivated and excited about what God has for you each and every day. You will look for what He is doing in your life and take the steps He gives you to walk into the future He has for you. You will live out of delight, not dread. Move boldly forward and trust the next chapter—when you know the author.

People who don't see a good future for themselves have no power in the present. They have no resilience, direction, perseverance, or drive. "Where there is no vision, the people perish . . ." (Prov. 29:18 KJV). They have nothing to look forward to, and they don't have any hope. So they retreat to their past and live there.

They may return to their past emotionally, rehearsing things they've done wrong, and never move forward. Or they may return to their past physically, back to their old homes, old neighborhood, and their old crowd. And when they go back, things are usually never what they thought they would be. So what is really back there? Nothing.

Have you ever experienced that? Have you thought that you could go back to a place in your past and it would be like it was when you left, but when you went there, you found it wasn't the same? This happened to Jesus's disciple, Peter.

When Peter first met Jesus, Peter and his brother, Andrew, both fishermen, were casting a net into the Sea of Galilee. Jesus, who was walking by the sea, said to them, ". . . 'Follow Me, and I will make you fishers of men.' They immediately left their nets and followed Him" (Matt. 4:18-19). After that, Jesus called two more disciples, and the four of them followed Jesus into their future. (vv. 21-22.)

They heard Jesus teach and preach and saw Him heal all kinds of sickness and diseases throughout Galilee. They saw Jesus's fame spread throughout Syria and witnessed Him healing those afflicted with various diseases and torments and the demon possessed, epileptics, and paralytics brought to Him. They were part of Jesus's ministry when great multitudes of people from many cities began following Him. (vv. 23-25.)

Jesus warned His disciples of what was coming: He would be killed and rise on the third day. (Mark 9:31.) "But they did not understand this saying and were afraid to ask Him" (v. 32). Jesus also said, ". . . 'I am going away and coming back to you'. . ." (John 14:28).

Peter and the other disciples were with Jesus when the events leading to Him "going away" began to unfold. The Jewish leaders had ". . . plotted to take Jesus by trickery and kill Him" (Matt. 26:3-4). Even though Jesus was innocent, He was betrayed by Judas, arrested, and taken away. (John 18:1-8, 12-13.) Then Jesus was crucified and died!

This was all part of God's plan for Jesus to die to take on all men's sins. But instead, He conquered death by rising from the dead to redeem humanity and create the way for those who would accept what He had done to form a relationship with God.

But to Peter, everything he had been living for was over. When Jesus was crucified and put into the tomb, Peter thought it was over. He gave up the cause. He felt as though he had no future. Instead, make sure you choose to live for what God has to offer you today, not what you believe yesterday has taken away.

Peter had pledged to Jesus, ". . . 'I will lay down my life for Your sake'" (John 13:37). But after Jesus was arrested, Peter refused to acknowledge that he knew Jesus, not only once, but three times. Jesus had told him he would do this: ". . . the rooster shall not crow till you have denied Me three times" (v. 38), and after Peter's denial, the rooster crowed. (Luke 22:60.) Peter had followed Jesus and those who had taken Him from a distance (v. 54), and ". . . the Lord turned and looked at Peter . . ." (v. 61). "So Peter went out and wept bitterly" (v. 62).

Peter had denied Christ! He felt like a failure. Everything was all over. Jesus was dead. But it wasn't over. What followed the crucifixion was the resurrection. Jesus rose from the dead!

Peter may have thought his future was to rule and reign over the Roman Empire with Jesus, but that was not God's plan. God had a different and better plan for Peter. So often, God takes us in another direction from the one we thought we would take to reach the end result, but God's plan is always better than our plan and of greater benefit to us and everyone affected!

Jesus rose from the dead and appeared to His disciples! Then, ". . . when the doors were shut where the disciples were assembled, for fear of the Jews, Jesus came and stood in the midst . . ." (John 20:19). But what did Peter do when he didn't think he had a future? He retreated, regressed, and returned to his past. He went back to his business, his career as a fisherman. But things didn't work out the way he had planned.

Peter thought he could pick up where he left off, but what did he find in his past? Nothing. He and some of the other disciples fished all night, but they didn't catch any fish. (John 21:3.) Even his business of the past, where he had been successful, was failing. It had shut down. He couldn't pick it back up. He couldn't move forward. It's easy to imagine how Peter felt—no good to God, no good to anybody, unloved, unaccepted, disqualified, not included, a mess-up, a has-been whose glory days were over, and a failure in every way.

But Jesus had the plan to restore Peter's future. When morning came, Jesus stood on the shore. The disciples didn't know who He was. After He asked them if they had any food (John 21:5), He told them, ". . . 'Cast the net on the right side of the boat, and you will find some . . .'" (v. 6a). They obeyed, cast the net, and caught so many fish, they were not able to draw in the catch. (John 21:6b.)

The disciples realized the man on the shore was Jesus! So they all made their way as quickly as possible to land to reach him. Jesus had prepared breakfast for them. (John 21:7-13.)

## JESUS HAS A GREAT FUTURE FOR US, AND IT ISN'T IN OUR PAST

After eating breakfast, Jesus talked to Peter (v. 15) and reminded him of the call on his life, purpose, and future. And He did it very interestingly to instruct Peter to move away from his past. So we see that Peter, who thought he was a failure, was restored.

> Jesus said, ". . . 'do you love Me more than these?'"
> Peter answered, ". . . 'Yes, Lord; You know that I love You.'"
> Jesus said to him, ". . . 'Feed My lambs'" (v. 15).

Then Jesus asked a second time. He was reminding Peter that God still had the same plan, assignment, destiny, and dream for Peter to fulfill in his life as he did before Jesus died.

Jesus said, ". . . 'do you love Me?'"

Peter answered, ". . . 'Yes, Lord; You know that I love You.'"

Jesus said to him, ". . . 'Tend My sheep'" (v. 16).

Then Jesus asked a third time.

Jesus said, ". . . 'do you love Me?'"

Peter answered, ". . . 'Lord, You know all things; You know that I love You."

Jesus said, "'Feed My sheep'" (v. 17).

Peter had denied Jesus three times, and Jesus reminded him of his call three times. It is significant that for each time of the denial, Jesus reminded Peter of the call in the future that God had on his life to be a pastor and a shepherd. Peter would show people on earth and in future generations the way to eternal life in relationship with the God who is for them.

*Stop stealing from your future with your past. It's over.*

Jesus told Peter that his call and future were the same as before. Jesus was removing all condemnation from Peter for being afraid and denying Him. He reminded Peter, "You're not a failure just because you failed. I won't cast you out because you denied Me. The mistakes that you've made, I'm not going to reject you for those. I'm reminding you of the future I have planned for you." Jesus was saying, "Don't let your past mistakes condemn you and stop you from moving forward." Stop stealing from your future with your past. It's over.

Then Jesus repeated Peter's purpose to him. When Jesus first met Peter, He said, ". . . 'Follow Me . . .'" (Matt. 4:19). And after Jesus rose from the dead, in restoring Peter's call, He said, ". . . 'Follow Me'" (John 21:19). The first thing Jesus said to Peter was, "Follow Me," and one of the last things He said to Peter was, "Follow Me." Jesus was saying nothing had changed for Peter. Jesus came and showed him how He brings success. Jesus was showing Peter to focus on his future. Then Peter did what He was supposed to do to walk into His future: he followed Jesus.

God's calling on our lives doesn't change. (Rom. 11:29.) God is for your future—that doesn't change. So we need not let our past stop us from going into the future God has planned for us.

Oswald Chambers said, "Leave the broken, irreversible past in God's hands, and step out into the invincible future with Him."

If you have a dream that looks dead and have no hope for the future, things may look like they're over, but they're not over. As Christ's followers, we go through a cycle of faith. There are times things get worse before they get better. It may look like our dream or our future has died, but often this is right before it is about to come alive. As we have seen, some people want to return to their past during those times. And if God didn't direct them to go there, what do they find? Like Peter, they find nothing. Things aren't the same as when they left. There's nothing there because Jesus has a great future for them, and it isn't their past. Jesus is done with their past, and they need to be done with it, too. Jesus wants them to keep following after Him and moving forward into the great future He has for them!

At one time, Kim and I went back to our past, although the reason was different from Peter's. But from there, we turned around and walked into our future.

When I first surrendered my life to God, Kim wasn't in the same place of realizing what He had planned for us. My search for meaning and purpose by acquiring everything I wanted had ended when I found only more unhappiness. Although at that point I didn't completely understand that God was for me and desired to lead me into good things, I quit running from Him. I had always known there was something He wanted me to do, and I was ready to follow Him and pursue whatever it was.

In those days, Kim and I spent a lot of time disagreeing. For example, when I told Kim we were going to Bible college, she said, "You are, but I'm not." I said, "I'm called to serve God." She answered, "You are, but I'm not."

But she went with me to Bible college! I drove us to a college in Minneapolis, Minnesota, and we were there for one year. She fought it the whole time. We quarreled. Sometimes when we were sitting in a class with other preachers, she would tell them, "I don't want to be here."

After a year, I couldn't take living like that anymore. I told God, "I love Kim and don't believe in divorce, so you will have to change Kim's heart. I can't. I've tried. It won't work."

We left school and returned to our hometown. I went into construction, leaving Kim's attitude and heart with God. Then something happened. At the end of the summer, Kim came to me and said, "You're right; I'm wrong. We're called. Let's go!" God had changed her heart!

*To make God bigger than your past, focus more on God than on your past.*

So we went to college in Texas and together began following God into the incredible future He had for us.

## MAKE GOD BIGGER THAN YOUR PAST

To make God bigger than your past, focus more on God than on your past. "The life in front of you is far more important than the life behind you," says my friend, Joel Osteen.

The things we focus on increase. If we focus on our problems, they get bigger in our eyes. If we focus on our past, our mistakes, failures, missed opportunities, and all the times we've messed up, we will start accepting the accuser's lies. We will believe that we're no good and will keep making the same mistakes or doing the same things that led to failure and never succeeding. People who focus on rehearsing the things they've done wrong will think they don't have a good future. They will retreat to their past emotionally and live there. They will never move into all God has for them.

Jesus was showing Peter that he should focus on Him rather than on his failure because what we focus on grows in our life.

When we focus on Jesus, we get our eyes off ourselves. When we focus on Him, we get our minds off our past sins, wrong choices, shortcomings, and the I-could-have-done-this and I-should-have-done-that scenarios.

Instead, we get our minds on knowing that, because of Jesus, our future is brighter than our past. We focus on God's goodness toward us and on Him being for us and moving for us. When we focus on God and His Word, our faith increases. We believe God will move on our behalf to accomplish everything He wants to do in our lives and future expansions. Jesus wants us to focus on our promising, prosperous future. We overcome our past when we know our future is bigger than our past. The famous old hymn by Helen Lemmel says it best, "Turn your eyes upon Jesus, Look full in His wonderful face, And the things of earth will grow strangely dim, In the light of His glory and grace."

Jesus encouraged Peter with His words because Peter was discouraged. Jesus was giving Peter faith for His future. We need to encourage ourselves with Jesus's words. Because "...faith comes by hearing, and hearing by the word of God" (Rom. 10:17), we need to feed our spirit with God's Word. Every time we read the Bible, our future should get bigger and brighter; we should get bolder and our belief system stronger.

## FOLLOW JESUS INTO YOUR FUTURE

Every day many things are pulling on us that we think we could or should do that day. We have many hats to wear, many responsibilities, and pressures. Many of us feel we've never been busier than we are now. But the most important thing Peter learned from Jesus that he could do if he wanted to move forward was to follow Jesus.

*If you follow Him, you'll find that the future He has for you will open up immediately.*

# GOD IS FOR YOU

You may find that the urgent things of the day often control your time. However, the most significant thing you could do today to move forward into God's plan for you is to make up your mind that you will follow Jesus. Doing so is not the most urgent thing, but it's the most important thing you could do for your marriage, family, child-rearing, business, ministry, career, and the decisions you need to make that are so pressing. If you follow Him, you'll find that the future He has for you will open up immediately.

Have your circumstances, or even your friends or your family, told you that things are over for you? Don't let anyone discourage you from doing what you know Jesus wants you to do. For example, instead of listening to the pastor who told me I didn't have what it takes to be in the ministry, I followed what I knew Jesus wanted me to do. And He took me where I was supposed to be, where Kim and I are able to minister the message of His goodness to thousands of people.

We can rise above our past. We can find and fulfill our future in Jesus.

Let Jesus increase in your life. Focus on Him. Focus on the God who is leading you into good things and moving for you even when everything looks like it's over. Focus on your future. Don't retreat to the past in your thoughts or physically. The past is where everything is over! "When the devil keeps asking you to look at your past, there's something in your future he doesn't want you to see" (Anonymous). Instead, feed yourself with the Word. And follow Jesus.

Jesus came to give you a victorious, thrilling, fulfilling, overcoming, adventurous life worth living. God is for your future, so walk boldly into the promising destiny He has for you today!

# 6

# YOUR FUTURE IS GOOD

## Discover God's Will for Your Life

"If there is hope in the future,

there is literally power in the present."

Zig Ziglar

God is for your future. Be excited, confident, and know that some of the best times of your life haven't happened yet.

Seeing the will of God for your future is like looking at a scroll, not a blueprint. When the scroll rolls back, you see a little bit. The future Kim and I are living in now, we didn't see as a blueprint. We didn't see the whole picture of how we would reach it. But we did see the end result. And God used that to empower our present.

God gave Kim and me a picture of the type of future we wanted when we visited The Jesus People Church in downtown Minneapolis the year we were there in college. Thousands and thousands of people of all types and racial backgrounds attended that church. Some people were dressed in shorts and flip-flops, others in expensive suits.

When you have a vision for your future, you see it and feel it. It's like test-driving a new car you may buy. The sales associate wants you to see the car and drive it so that you feel it, smell it, and buy it. He or she wants to tie the vehicle to your emotions. The experience at The Jesus People Church tied the emotion of pastoring a church like it to my vision for our future. This was in 1976. Even though Kim wasn't on board with our vision yet, I looked at her and said, "I want a church like this. I just saw my future."

*Be more committed to God's will than you are to staying in your comfort zone.*

That day in Minneapolis, we saw the vision of the exciting future God had for us. In pursuing our future in God, we saw the end at the beginning, but we didn't see all the steps in between. We reached that future by taking one step at a time, the next step, then the next that God revealed as He rolled back the scroll. We figured it out as we went along, following Him on the great adventure, anticipating where He would take us next!

That vision came to pass with our church we planted nearly forty years ago, Church on the Rock. All types of people from all walks of life, culturally, socially, and economically, attend the church, including multimillionaires, people working through financial issues, and those whose life experiences are at different stages between those two. Many educators and engineers attend. Across the street we have a Spanish church, Church on the Rock Español, and we broadcast a Spanish TV program there.

Be more committed to God's will than you are to staying in your comfort zone. That's one of the reasons we're starting a campus in the metaverse for our services. Everyone will have an avatar to interact with other people. I'll have an avatar, as well as the people on our worship team.

We've been testing the metaverse campus. The person who handles our IT began creating small groups in it. Because people have avatars, they tend to be more open, honest, and receptive. It's incredible to watch this because they hide behind their avatars. Recently after our IT tech went into a chat room, which was one of the small groups he had designed, he said, "Pastor, you wouldn't believe how open these people are. The other night, I was talking to a guy in the chat room who came out and said, 'I'm an atheist, but I'm open. Tell me why you have a relationship with God.'"

The metaverse ministry is opening up a whole new mission field. Metaverse is without borders. We can reach anybody anywhere with it. People can interact directly on this platform and, if they desire, feel anonymous. Metaverse provides the opportunity to reach many people who are open, receptive, searching, and looking for more, like the atheist was. We are seeing so many people open up who want to hear a positive message, and we can minister Jesus to them on a personal level. The average age of people attending Church on the Rock is thirty-nine or forty. The metaverse draws in slightly younger people. It fits right into their world.

Our church is a representation of the cross section of people in America. It looks like America. This is the type of church we wanted and what God gave us.

How did we know what specific steps to take to fulfill the vision of a church of five thousand we dreamed about in college to become the reality of more than six thousand in the church we have today?

Many people ask that type of question. How do I know if the potential steps I see to take are from God? How exactly do I know what specific steps to take—whether to do one thing rather than another? How do I know what those steps are?

*God has specific answers for those questions we have for Him.*

How do I know specifically what I should do with my life, career, job, business, or ministry? Should I marry a particular person I'm dating? What car or house should I purchase? Where should we send our kids to school? Should I say yes to a person asking me to do something or say no to a move? What should I do in different situations I encounter just walking through my day? I want to hear from God and know His direction in these things. When I'm considering what to do, I want to hear: do this, don't do that.

How does my relationship with God work? How do I cooperate with Him? How do I position myself for God to move in a mighty way for me? How do I know what God wants me to do? How do I know God's will in any situation?

How do I know God's will for my life? Greg Laurie says, "God's plans for you are better than any plans you have for yourself. So don't be afraid of God's will, even if it's different from yours."

God has specific answers for those questions we have for Him.

## GOD HAS A SPECIFIC WILL FOR EACH OF US

First, we must understand that God has a will for our life; a purpose, a destiny, for each of us. We saw that Romans 8:28 refers to being "... called according to His purpose," and Ephesians 2:10 tells us we are "... created in Christ Jesus for good works, which God prepared beforehand that we should walk in them."

The wording in *The Message* version of Ephesians 1:11-12 describes God as specifically designing a life for each of us. "It's in Christ that we find out who we are and what we are living for. Long before we first heard of Christ and got our hopes up, he had his eye on us, had designs on us for glorious living, part of the overall purpose he is working out in everything and everyone."

Specially designed things on earth have more value. For example, designer jeans, shirts, or purses are specially made and cost more. This is similar to the way God looks at us: God has a life of great value specifically designed for us, a designer life for each of us.

To achieve our goals in anything we do in life, we give up some things; we sacrifice some things to reach our goals. It's the same with following God's will for our lives. Without surrender or sacrifice, there can be limited success. But the end result is even more rewarding than we could have anticipated. Sacrifice is part of every journey to being all God wants you to be.

We know from Matthew 16:24 that Jesus said to His disciples, ". . . 'If any of you wants to be my follower, you must give up your own way, take up your cross, and follow me'" (NLT). This means for us the same as it meant for the disciples—to give up our desires for God's desires in our life. God's plan never leaves you empty. If He directs you to put something down, it's because He has something better for you to pick up.

It isn't until we let go and die to our desires that we discover all the good that Jesus has for us. It is a blessed life. We lay down our life, lose our life, to find our life. We let go to discover. Jesus said, "'For whoever desires to save his life will lose it, but whoever loses his life for My sake will find it'" (Matt. 16:25). We begin to discover the blessed life God made for us and wants us to live. We lay down our life by surrendering to what God wants us to do and sacrificing what we want to do. The result that comes from obeying, surrendering, and sacrificing along the way brings the best for us. Discover the joy of giving up what we want to the One we love the most.

Many people don't want to surrender their will to God's will because they think their lives will be inferior to the life they could have had. They believe it will be a less satisfying life, boring. However, the life of following Jesus is not boring. Getting born again, giving our lives to Christ, surrendering, sacrificing what we think we want to do for what He wants us to do, being steadfast, and clinging to Him leads us to a blessed life.

We saw in Ephesians 1:11-12 that God already had devised His wonderful plan for us long before we heard of Christ. Hearing of Christ gets our hopes up according to the interpretation of this passage in *The Message*, which paraphrases the Bible in contemporary language. Through Christ, we find out who we are and what we are living for, and hearing of Him should get our hopes up!

*Following God's will for our lives is the safest place to be in a hostile world.*

For people feeling completely hopeless about life, discovering who they are in Christ and why they're here brings hope.

## DISCOVER GOD'S WILL FOR YOU

Everyone needs to feel significant. If we're not in God's will, we won't reach our potential or tap into our true significance. We won't ever feel content, happy, satisfied, and fulfilled. And if we are in God's will, in the midst of all the turmoil in the world today, we are in a safe place. Following God's will for our lives is the safest place to be in a hostile world.

Jesus left heaven and came to earth to do one thing. His priority and purpose were to fulfill God's will. He said, ". . . 'Behold, I have come...To do Your will, O God'" (Heb. 10:7). We are on the earth for the same reason: to fulfill God's will.

Knowing God's purpose for our lives and fulfilling it should be a priority; it should be the most important thing in our life. But it is our responsibility to discover it. We don't determine it; we discover God's will for our life. It's up to us. We use our initiative and drive and are intentional about finding the answer to the question: "God, why am I here?" We discover His will and develop and distribute it.

Just as Jesus was "moved with compassion" (Matt. 14:14 KJV), we will be moved with compassion to distribute what we know about God. Many people who don't know Jesus or know how much He is for them are struggling. People are perishing in their sins. Homes are broken. Lives are shattered. Multitudes are bewildered, harassed, distressed, dejected, and helpless. We will know how to move in God's love to help people find the answers they need and discover God's purpose for them. God's will includes helping others. There are souls attached to your gifts and calling. As a follower of Jesus, we make another follower of Jesus, then make more. We show others how to know God, experience all the good He has for them, and live the fulfilling life they would have thought impossible.

Jesus is looking for people who will say, as Isaiah the prophet said, ". . . 'Here am I! Send me'" (Isa. 6:8). God is not looking for ability so much as availability. He is looking for faithful, available, and teachable people. No matter what God's will is for us, we know His will for all of us is to love with His love.

## LIVING IN GOD'S WILL

Before I surrendered to God's will for my life, I was miserable, empty, and going nowhere. On the outside, I looked like I was on the way to being even more successful. I looked like I should have been happy, but on the inside, I was not satisfied or secure. I was not safe. It's a requirement to surrender to God's will in your life because He will lead you to the places He knows are best for you. But you must be willing to submit to what He tells you to do to reach them.

After giving my life to God for Him to guide me, I didn't know exactly what His will was for me. I knew only that I had to find meaning in my life and that whatever He had for me, I didn't want to be average. That first step toward discovering His will for me was knowing I needed to go to college. I learned the purpose He had for me later. I followed Him step-by-step as He rolled back the scroll.

How do you discover your personal purpose, your calling? First, think about your abilities and skills. The way God designed you reveals your purpose in life and your best fit in ministry. And very important: think about your dream. What is your dream? What is the desire of your heart? You will probably find that your personal vision is that thing you think about that's tied to your emotions and won't go away. You may forget about it at times, but then it comes back. It's persistent. As long as it is in agreement with the teaching in God's Word, explore it as God's direction.

After Kim and I left college in Minneapolis, we went back to our hometown. I started working in construction, but the vision was still there. It never went away. Then at the end of the summer, both Kim and I were ready to launch full force into taking God's steps toward pursuing it.

We had taken a detour on the way to discovering our future.

## EXPECT DETOURS

It won't always be a straight line you follow when moving toward the goal. Instead, there may be detours on the way to your destination of living in the future God has for you. Ask God to show you His will, way, and time.

Or you may be sidetracked on the way to your destination. Have you ever set your goal, felt sure that God was leading you, and suddenly got sidetracked? This happens often. There may be potholes, unexpected events, and results of things that happen, even from your own wrong decisions, to slow you down.

If you make a mistake on your way to your future, and you will, you need to get up and keep going. Of course, you will stumble along at times, but in whatever you're going through today, do as David did: be open to God. (Ps. 139:23.) Let Him search you and talk to you. Say to Him, "God, search me and show me who I need to become. Show me how I can get there."

If you caused a detour by making a wrong decision, have the mindset that if you're not making mistakes, you're not learning. We need to keep learning. Remain a student in every challenge. Learn in the storm.

John C. Maxwell said, "If you're not failing, you're probably not really moving forward."

In my church, we've learned more from our losses than our wins. Growing never ends. We're lifelong learners. We see every disappointment as an appointment. Yesterday's surprises are today's opportunities. Many times when we experienced something that looked terrible, we saw it turn into something good. Surprises were actually one of our biggest opportunities for ministry going forward.

There will be times of following God and pushing through discouragement. Many times, at the moment, it may not look as though anything is happening for the good. I've discovered many times if God is causing you to wait, then be prepared to receive more than you asked for.

> *I've discovered many times if God is causing you to wait, then be prepared to receive more than you asked for.*

Sometimes when people are detoured, they think the detour is the end. They believe the detour is an unsurpassable roadblock that means God isn't with them or for them. But God is for them. He has a strategy for every challenge, limitation, and success. What they need to do is adjust, adapt, and keep being obedient.

When Kim and I left college and went back to our past, the future God had for us wasn't there. I knew I was still called to the ministry, but I retreated because the way I was trying to get there wasn't working. In this case, returning to our past was a detour on the way to the place God had for us to go. However, God was working to turn everything around for our good. And from that point, Kim and I were in complete agreement and excited to follow God together into our future.

Detours, distractions, and surprises are usually part of the process. And God has a way around or through them all. He will come through in amazing ways at just the right time. Kim and I have been on detours and sidetracked many times. But we still reached our goal and are living in the exceptional future God had planned for us.

When you are detoured, apply everything you know to do to keep believing that God is working for you. Don't be discouraged. Take action. Instead of accepting the accuser's lies, declare the truth in God's Word over your situation and destiny. Keep believing that the all-knowing, ever-present, and all-powerful God is working for you to bring you overwhelming victory! And keep doing what you see He has for you to do. You will watch Him move in a mighty way to take you into your destiny as you follow Him step by specific step.

# 7

# YOUR FUTURE IS GOOD

## WALK INTO THE FUTURE GOD HAS FOR YOU, ONE STEP AT A TIME

Living in God's will for our lives is the most productive and prolific place we can be. As we saw in the previous chapters, we don't design the plan God has for us; we don't determine what we are to do with our lives, we discover it. And God has specific steps ordered for us to fulfill that plan. He brings our unique destiny into the present when we follow Him.

God gives us the steps in the order He wants us to take them to walk into that plan. His Word tells us, "The steps of a good man are ordered by the Lord . . ." (Ps. 37:23). Another wording of this verse states, "The Lord directs the steps of the godly . . ." (NLT). Although God gives us the steps to take to fulfill our purpose, we may miss a step and go off course at times. But we know to stay focused on Jesus; He will show us where we need to go.

We fulfill God's plan for us by taking one step at a time. Everything big starts with something small. And God does lead us in steps, not leaps. When Kim and I birthed Church on the Rock nearly forty years ago on a holiday, thirty-five people attended. Our attendance grew from thirty-five to more than six thousand, one step at a time, one day at a time—in steps, not leaps.

How did Kim and I know the specific steps God wanted us to take to walk into our future? And how will you know which actions He wants you to take to fulfill your destiny?

THE LORD MAY DIRECT YOU IN UNEXPECTED WAYS

We make plans, but God may have different plans for taking us where He wants us to go. "A man's heart plans his way, but the Lord directs his steps" (Prov. 16:9). As we follow Him, we discover He is taking us to the place where we also want to go. In Jeremiah 10:23, we saw that we have "limited ability" compared to God's ability (AMP) to choose the correct steps. Because God knows the future He has for us, He knows the best way for us to reach it!

*Choose God's will in God's way.*

When the Lord leads us in a direction we hadn't expected, we need to follow the advice in Proverbs 3:5-6: "Trust in the Lord with all your heart; do not depend on your own understanding. Seek his will in all you do, and he will show you which path to take" (NLT). The *New King James Version* words this passage, ". . . lean not on your own understanding; in all your ways acknowledge Him, and He shall direct your paths." God leads where we need to be, not always where we want to be. Trust that He has the best in store for you, and let Him take you there!

Stay open to what God is saying to you. This means to submit and surrender to His direction and steps rather than taking the path you think is best. We can't determine the most effective way to achieve our vision for maximum benefit to ourselves and others, but God has it planned. Craig Groeschel says, "You don't have to understand the plan to trust that God has a purpose." Choose God's will in God's way.

God illuminates our way. "Your word is a lamp to my feet and a light to my path . . ." (Ps. 119:105). Kim and I know the reality of living Psalm 119:105. We followed the steps God illuminated for us. I believe we can say that God leaves the "lights on for us."

One of the two churches we first pastored had eleven members. After we began pastoring that church, it grew. Its membership increased dramatically and quickly. The other church we pastored started with fifty members, and we also saw its membership explode.

Kim and I were ready to plant our church in a larger community. Three different groups of people from three cities approached us. Each group wanted us to start our church in their area. We needed to choose the right place where God had the best plans for us and the people the church would reach. God doesn't want us to have His second best; He wants us to have His best—the good life, the blessed life. We knew how to seek Him to learn which city He wanted us to choose.

## GREEN, YELLOW, OR RED

There are several signals to look for that indicate we are moving in the direction God wants for us and we are in line with His will. These signals are like the ones at a traffic light: green, yellow, or red. If the traffic signal's light is green, that's a go light. You go to the next signal, the next step in the process. If that next signal is green, you go

*The voice of God's Word gives us the green light.*

to the signal after it. As long as the signal is green, you keep proceeding down the road to the next step. Finally, at the last signal, if all the signals have been green, you know you're in God's perfect will. So, keep moving forward in that direction.

## THE VOICE OF GOD'S WORD

### Is the step in line with the teaching in the Word?

God's Word is His will. First, we have to have confirmation from Scripture that the action we're taking is biblically accurate. The step we are considering must be in line with the teaching in the Word. When it is, this is the first indication, the first signal, that we are moving in the direction God has for us. The voice of God's Word gives us the green light. This provides us with the confidence and assurance to move boldly ahead.

To know if the step we are about to take agrees with the Word, we need to know what the Word says! We do this by reading the Word regularly, every day.

More than seven thousand promises in the Bible show us how much God is for us. For example, John 10:10 tells us that Jesus came to give us life and life more abundantly. (KJV.) It is God's will, according to the Word, for us to have an abundantly good life, a blessed life. The Word shows us that God wants us to succeed. (Prov. 16:3 AMPC, NLT; Ps. 90:17 NKJV, NLT; Prov. 22:4.)

We saw in Psalm 68:19 that the Lord "daily loads us with benefits." Psalm 103:2-5 tells us not to forget His benefits: forgiveness, healing, redemption from destruction, and renewed youth. He crowns us ". . . with lovingkindness, and tender mercies" (v. 4)—love, kindness, and mercy. To know who we are, what we have, what we can do, and all that God has available to us, we need to know His promises by studying the Word. We need to know and claim them for our lives, and receive, embrace, and enjoy them.

God wants you to be blessed in every area. He wants you to succeed with your health, job, and career; in your marriage, parenting, and raising your kids for Him—He wants you to succeed and experience His best in life! No matter what direction you see the world going around you, God wants to guide you into the abundantly promising future He has for you.

Hosea 4:6 tells us, "My people are destroyed for lack of knowledge . . ." So if we are doing something that is not in line with the Word because we are unfamiliar with its instruction in that particular area, we are out of God's will without knowing it.

First John 5 tells us that God hears and answers us when we ask in agreement with His will, which is His Word. "Now this is the confidence that we have in Him, that if we ask anything according to His will, He hears us. And if we know that He hears us, whatever we ask, we know that we have the petitions that we have asked of Him" (vv. 14-15).

We need to ask in line with the Word because if we ask outside of the Word, we're outside of God's will. If we're not in God's will or His plan, there is no promise that He will listen to or grant our requests. For example, twenty-five or thirty years ago, a lady attending our church told me she believed God wanted her to marry a particular usher in our church. However, this was not God's will because the usher was already married! Her plan didn't agree with God's Word; therefore, it wasn't God's will. She had no scriptural basis to believe God wanted her to marry somebody who was already married. This is an extreme illustration, but it shows the importance of knowing God's will through knowing His Word on a particular subject.

When we have Scripture to stand on, God's Word speaks to us. We're assured that what we're asking, seeking, and petitioning for is in line with God's Word and His will. We know to move confidently ahead on the road He has for us. The God, who is for us, will bring our good future to pass! "God's will is found in God's Word. Stop looking for a sign and start looking for a verse," says Pastor Rick Warren.

There are many voices in the world today. There are voices of unbelief, fear, and doubt. There are many voices offering choices that disagree with the voice of God's Word. There is evil behind many of these trying to lead us in a way that will turn out badly for us and keep us from fulfilling our purpose and affecting people for Jesus. Jesus said, "My sheep hear my voice, and I know them, and they follow me" (John 10:27 KJV). We know we hear Jesus's voice when it lines up with the teaching in the Word. As His sheep, we need to make sure we hear His voice and take action based on the voice of the Word. When we know what God's Word says, we have the voice of the Word speaking to us.

God gives us direction in His Word to bless us and others through us. A talebearer, who maliciously hurts people by gossiping and spreading rumors on social media, is not acting in line with the instructions in God's Word. Someone living with someone else and having an intimate relationship without being married, or someone who is not working when fully capable of having a job or building a career, is not functioning in line with the voice of God's Word. We need to go to the Word and make sure that what we are doing agrees with it. We build the house of our lives on the Rock and the good that God has for us and those we influence by living in line with the voice of His Word and walking in agreement with His will.

*Train your mind to listen to what His Spirit whispers, not what the world is shouting.*

## THE VOICE OF THE HOLY SPIRIT

**Follow peace.**

When we receive Jesus, the Holy Spirit lives in us. As God's children, we can listen to the Holy Spirit's voice and be led by Him. "For all who are led by the Spirit of God are children of God" (Rom. 8:14 NLT).

Someone may be thinking, *How do I do that? This is all new to me. How do I know the voice I'm hearing is the Holy Spirit's voice?*

As we grow up spiritually by learning God's Word and submitting to it, we develop our human spirit so that we hear the Holy Spirit's voice speaking to our spirit inside of us. We get to know the Holy Spirit and how He operates so that we are working with Him and not against Him—not against what He wants to do in and through us. We learn how to hear His voice and follow His leading. Train your mind to listen to what His Spirit whispers, not what the world is shouting. We are not led by our circumstances or emotions, but by the Holy Spirit.

His "voice" is often an impression. For example, you may have had a feeling, or an impression, that you should have driven a different way to work but didn't and were caught in a traffic jam for an hour. Or, when you abide in a place of listening for the Holy Spirit's voice, you may have had an impression that you should say something specific to someone. You did and learned that what you said was exactly what the person needed to hear.

We need to be sure the impression is from the Holy Spirit. One way we know we are hearing the Holy Spirit's voice is that we experience peace. Colossians 3:15 tells us to let the peace ". . . from Christ rule (act as umpire continually) in your hearts . . ." (AMPC).

The Holy Spirit acts as an umpire does in a baseball game. One of the umpires stands behind the catcher. Based on the rules, he makes certain calls on the plays, such as "Safe" or "Out."

When you ask for the Holy Spirit's direction, you are asking Him to lead you. His direction is always in line with the teaching in the Word, but you're asking because you need to know how to handle specific situations. You have questions about decisions and choices you need to make. You need answers. Colossians 3:15 continues by saying that letting the peace from Christ rule in your heart and act as an umpire is ". . . [deciding and settling with finality all questions that arise in your minds . . ." (AMPC).

This tells us that the Holy Spirit will answer the questions we have for Him.

We let the peace of God be the umpire to decide and answer all questions that arise in our minds by waiting for that peace to come inside of us. Some people call it a confident assurance, a quickening on the inside that, yes, this is the correct answer. Or if the answer is no, because the solution does not bring peace, they feel checked from going forward and say, "I've got a check in my spirit."

The peace of Christ, to those of us who believe in Him, is always available when determining which direction the Holy Spirit is leading. John 14:27 tells us Jesus gave us His peace. (KJV.) Letting the peace from Christ rule in our hearts means we can live moment by moment according to the direction that peace gives us.

At this second traffic signal when you're asking the Holy Spirit, "Is the step I'm planning safe or out? Should I do this?", wait for the answer and the peace to come. That peace is the green light to move ahead to the next signal.

Colossians 3:15 ends with ". . . And be thankful (appreciative), [giving praise to God always] . . ." (AMPC). We are to always be thankful, appreciative, and expressive of our gratitude by giving God praise. In this verse, we see one of the many reasons we have for being very grateful: we believers in Jesus have an edge on the world because the Holy Spirit leads us in making the right decisions!

If you are unable to receive guidance from the Holy Spirit because He does not live in you, make the first right decision to accept and believe in Jesus. There is so much God has for you and so much good He wants to do for you!

Begin on that path into your incredible future with God by allowing the Holy Spirit to live in and lead you. Believe that Jesus died to take your sins that separated you from forming a relationship with God. Accept Jesus as the way to spend eternity with God starting now on earth to experience hearing the Holy Spirit's voice and living by His guidance. Don't stand in the way of what God wants to do! Have an edge on the world and walk in the blessed life He has for you.

## PEACE ABOUT ST. LOUIS

Kim and I let the Holy Spirit guide us in deciding which of the three cities we should choose to live in and birth our church. We listened to His voice and let Jesus's peace rule as the umpire in making the decision. At first, we didn't have a clear peace about which city to choose. But the more we prayed, the more peace we had about St. Louis.

We didn't have that peace when we prayed about the other two cities. We didn't feel right about either one. We weren't excited at the thought of starting the church in either town. Kim and I had that check in our spirit telling us not to proceed in either of those directions. The Holy Spirit, the umpire, was saying, "Out!" We had a red light.

As we continued to pray about St. Louis, the peace grew stronger and stronger. The umpire was saying, "Safe! It's My will. Go to St. Louis." Finally, we had the green light. We knew we were to choose St. Louis.

We wanted the perfect will of God, not the merely acceptable this-is-good-to-get-us-by will, for our lives. We wanted God's best. And He gave us His best. God wants the best for you, too.

God wants to guide you with the voice of His Word and the voice of the Holy Spirit. The Holy Spirit is your ". . . Helper (Comforter, Advocate, Intercessor—Counselor, Strengthener, Standby) . . ." (John 14:26 AMP). He is ready to lead and help you. God has His part—He wants to lead us very specifically—and we have our part—to listen

*To bring your future into your today, you need to get moving.*

for His voice and take the steps He gives us. And when we hear Him, we need to take action.

## GET MOVING

To bring your future into your today, you need to get moving. Action is mediocrity's worst enemy. God can't steer a parked car. If you're unsure what step in the process God has for you, go ahead and move toward an area that interests you. If it isn't for you, you'll find out. Sometimes, you discover what you're not supposed to do by taking action. The signal will turn red. And you won't spend the rest of your life wondering whether you should have pursued something you never did. You'll know. You'll find out if that direction is not the way you should go. Driving toward that step may have taken you on a little detour, but, as we saw, detours are to be expected along the way. Redirect yourself and keep going to get on the main road God has for you.

If you take that step and the signal is green, you'll know it is the right way and to keep moving in that direction. You'll be on your way to experiencing a part of the plan and an important part of your life that you might have otherwise completely missed.

God has something for you to do every day to impact the destiny He has for you. What can you do next week or today to get going? What is the next small action you can take? Move out toward the future God has for you, and watch what He does to take you there!

# 8

# YOUR FUTURE IS GOOD

## Keep Following the Green Lights

God has the kind of success in store for you beyond any you could imagine when you keep following the green lights and walking according to His will! Proverbs 16:3 (NLT) tells us our plans will succeed when we commit our actions to the Lord. This verse has saved me from making many bad decisions.

The *Amplified Bible, Classic Edition* version of this verse gives us more insight into how to commit our actions to the Lord: "Roll your works upon the Lord [commit and trust them wholly to Him; He will cause your thoughts to become agreeable to His will, and] so shall your plans be established and succeed." You and I are not responsible for trying to figure everything out. We're here to trust God that He already has.

# GOD IS FOR YOU

## TRUST THE GOD WHO IS FOR YOU

We roll our works upon the Lord and trust them to Him by believing that God is working for us and wants to bring us success. As we saw in previous chapters, when we love God and are called according to His purpose, we know that He causes everything to work together for our good. (Rom. 8:28.)

Psalm 55:22 says, "Cast your burden on the Lord [releasing the weight of it] . . ." (AMPC). This means to unload your burdens on the Lord—the actions you are taking, concerns about uncertainty in your future, questions, and present set of circumstances. All of your anxieties you roll, unload, on Him by trusting that He will work in those specific circumstances, no matter how bad they look, to bring the best for you out of them.

You can give all your worries to God because He cares about and for you. He bears your burdens and loads you with benefits daily, and He will sustain you. (1 Peter 5:7 NLT, AMP, NIV; Ps. 68:19 NIV, NKJV; Ps. 55:22 NIV, NLT, AMPC; Ps. 37:5 NLT, NKJV.) Trusting God to work in all our circumstances and taking each step by faith helps us press through fear into receiving all God has for us. So, give God your worries. He's going to be up all night anyway.

## YOUR PLANS WILL SUCCEED

Again, Proverbs 16:3 tells us that when we roll our works on the Lord, committing them to Him, He causes our thoughts to become agreeable to His will and our plans to be established and succeed.

*God wants to give us the desires of our heart.*

This is a significant, huge revelation: when you commit and trust your works to the Lord, He will cause your thoughts to become agreeable to His will. When your thoughts are agreeable to His will, your desires agree with His desires. You will make decisions in line with His will because your heart's desires have become His. Your choices in line with His desires will bring about the best for you because He desires the best for you, so your plans will be established and succeed. Your plans will succeed!

God wants to give us the desires of our heart: "Delight yourself also in the Lord, and He will give you the desires and secret petitions of your heart" (Ps. 37:4 AMPC). When we are sold out to God and put Him first, He puts His desires in our heart, and He sees to it that they come to pass: "Commit your way to the Lord, trust also in Him, and He shall bring it to pass" (v. 5).

In the book of Nehemiah, we read an account of God putting a desire in Nehemiah's heart and fulfilling it.

A Jew living in Persia and King Artaxerxes's cupbearer, Nehemiah, learned the wall of Jerusalem had been broken down and its gates burned with fire. When he heard the city was lying in waste, Nehemiah sat down and wept. He mourned for many days, fasting, and praying. Yet, Nehemiah was committed to the Lord. He cast his burden on the Lord, prayed, and had a plan, God's plan! God put the desire to rebuild the wall of Jerusalem in Nehemiah's heart. And God brought the desire to pass! (Neh. 1:2-4, 11; 2:3, 12; 6:15.)

Nehemiah had great favor with Artaxerxes. At Nehemiah's request, the king sent him to Judah to accomplish his plan; he gave him letters to the governors of the regions beyond the Euphrates River to let him pass through and a letter to the keeper of the king's forest to supply him with timber. The king also sent captains of the army and horsemen with him. (Neh. 2:5-9 AMPC.) "And the king granted what I asked, for the good hand of my God was upon me" (Neh. 2:8 AMPC).

Nehemiah encountered and overcame significant opposition. When enemies heard the wall was being rebuilt, they mocked the Jews and plotted together to attack Jerusalem and cause injury, confusion, and failure. (Neh. 4:1-3, 7-8, 11 AMPC.) Some of Nehemiah's nobles and officials were exacting interest from their relatives, interest which was forbidden, driving the people into deep poverty. (Neh. 5:1-7, 10 AMPC.) But Nehemiah knew the work God had given him to do and that God would accomplish the task through him. He frustrated the enemies' plans and rebuked the nobles and officials, demanding they provide restoration. (Neh. 4:9-23; 5:1-11 AMPC.)

Through prayer, wise strategy (Neh. 4:4-5, 9), and his admonishment to the people, ". . . 'Do not be afraid of them. Remember the Lord, great and awesome, and fight for your brethren, your sons, your daughters, your wives, and your houses'" (v. 14), Nehemiah saw God bring the plot of the enemy to nothing. (v. 15.)

Nehemiah persisted in leading his equally determined people, who ". . . had a heart and mind to work" (v. 6 AMPC), through to victory. The heart desire God had given Nehemiah was of great significance to Nehemiah and the future of the Jews who had been living in distress and reproach without a wall around Jerusalem. (Neh. 1:3.) And God brought the desire to pass. Nehemiah finished the wall! (Neh. 6:15.)

The great and awesome God fulfilled Nehemiah's desire and displayed His glory. "And it happened, when all our enemies heard of it, and all the nations around us saw these things, that they were very disheartened in their own eyes; for they perceived that this work was done by our God" (v. 16).

As we take the steps God gives us to fulfill our destiny, we know to expect detours. Trust that He is leading you somewhere. Have faith in His purpose. Still, we will also encounter opposition from people, circumstances, and sometimes ourselves if we don't keep our vision before us and remind ourselves of who we are in God and the good He wants to do for us and through us. We must remember that we are in a spiritual fight, and because of discouraging circumstances, we may think everything we are working toward is over for us, as Peter did after Jesus died. But we know to rehearse the truth that God wants to bring us overwhelming victory.

Focus on your knowledge of who God is and what He does that you have learned. Keep renewing your mind to the Word so that you may know God's good and pleasing and perfect will for you. (Rom. 12:2 KJV, NLT.) Remember that meditating on the Word will change the way you think! (v. 2 NLT.) Filling your mind with God's Word leaves no room for other negative thoughts. Speak verses aloud that have given you the proper perspective of God. Keep confessing God is good and working on your behalf. Do your best to have your actions and words agree with each other. Don't succumb to the enemy's lies and accept anything he tells you otherwise! Like Nehemiah, keep pressing through and working toward accomplishing the plan.

Charles R. Swindoll said, "Vision is the ability to see God's presence, to perceive God's power, to focus on God's plan in spite of the obstacles."

## THE VOICE OF YOUR HEART'S DESIRE

**Is the step something you have the desire to do?**

The voice of your heart's desire is the third traffic signal indicating whether we are proceeding according to God's will. When your desires are in line with God's good plan for your life, His will, He grants you the desires of your heart.

Will the step you're considering fulfill a desire of your heart as it did in the example of Nehemiah? Nehemiah had committed his works to God and prayed. He knew His desire was from God before he moved ahead. And before we pursue the desire we have in our hearts, we need to make sure it is God's desire, not ours. We need to check our thoughts and determine whether emotions or the peace from God is leading us.

When you know your desire is in line with the teaching in God's Word, and you have peace about pursuing it, and you've committed your works and way to God, and you're sure your desire is His desire, you will see that the third traffic signal you approach will be green. So move ahead to the next signal.

# GOD IS FOR YOU

## GOD IS FOR YOUR SUCCESS

Proverbs 16:3 has saved me from a lot of heartaches by keeping my decisions in line with God's desires for me. I have made many dumb decisions, but I could have made many more if it hadn't been for this verse. God's desires have become my desires; His plans have become my plans, and they succeed.

Years ago, when our boys were small, one of my heart's desires was to buy a bass fishing boat. We liked going fishing. I thought it would be great to have a boat to take on a family outing. We wanted to go out on a lake north of where we lived. So I began watching for a bass boat to purchase.

Kim and I came across one when we were driving and had stopped at an intersection. A guy had his bass boat for sale right there. So I said, "Kim, look, there's a used bass boat for sale. I want to check it out."

We pulled in by the boat, and I called the number on the sign. The owner had his business across the street, so I walked over there and talked to him. He wanted a certain amount for the boat and wouldn't negotiate for a lower price. "Take it or leave it," he said, then talked about the boat's different features. "It will make you a good boat."

I told him I was going to talk to my wife. I walked back to the car and said to Kim, "Oh, this is God. It's His will for us to have this boat." Sometimes we try to convince someone else that something is God's will because we want it so much at the time. I said, "Think of the family time and how we're going to grow closer out on the lake. It will bring relief from stress in the ministry. And can you imagine the bass?" My heart's desire was in line with God's desire, but I was going about fulfilling it according to my plan, not His. My plan would have brought a mediocre result. His plan got the best result.

Kim said, "Let's pray about it." I said, "Okay, but I'm excited about it. I know it's God's will. It's perfect."

That night the owner called me and offered a lower price.

I told Kim, "The guy just went down on the price. I know it's definitely God's will now. I can't wait till tomorrow to call him back." She said, "Just give it a little time. Let's pray about it."

Instead of contacting the man right away, I did what Kim said and waited another day. Then I waited a second day. And by the third day, I wasn't as excited about that boat as I had been at first. It wasn't God's perfect will for us to have it. If I had gone ahead with my impulse of buying instead of listening for the Holy Spirit's voice, we would have been in God's permissive will, permitted but not exceptional. We would have missed God's best in fulfilling my heart's desire because we later acquired a brand-new Ranger bass boat!

What a blessing it was. God didn't want us to buy the used bass boat because He was preparing a top-of-the-line new boat for us, a type that fulfilled my heart's desire more than I had imagined. God's desire for us became my desire, and I waited for His outcome. His plan was a little different from mine, but the reason was that it brought a better result. God's desire was for us to have the best bass boat.

> When we already know our purpose and have it in our hearts, God gives us smaller desires along the way to build the practical basis for accomplishing the more significant desire.

I had committed my actions to the Lord and, thanks to Kim's wise suggestions, waited for the Holy Spirit's peace, which I never received. The traffic signal was red. Then my desire became God's desire, to wait for the right boat. And God brought my desire to pass in a way that demonstrated Ephesians 3:20: it was exceedingly abundantly above all that I had thought or imagined.

# GOD IS FOR YOU

## FULFILLING THE VISION THROUGH SPECIFIC DESIRES

When we already know our purpose and have it in our hearts, God gives us smaller desires along the way to build the practical basis for accomplishing the more significant desire.

In college, Kim and I already knew our purpose. We both had the heart desire to start a church that would minister to thousands of people. But, at that time, we didn't know exactly how, when, or where God would fulfill that dream. But, once we began taking our first few steps, He directed us toward fulfilling our bigger heart desire by giving us a specific heart desire and showing us the location. The future you create depends upon the deliberate choices you make and the particular actions you take.

After college, we began taking the beginning steps God gave us toward fulfilling our purpose by serving and pastoring in already existing churches. Then we knew it was time to take specific action to go out on our own and start the church.

The peace and excitement we experienced over God's direction to start the church in St. Louis became a specific heart desire that gave us the first significant practical step toward accomplishing our overall desire, our purpose. After we had moved forward through the first two green traffic lights, we saw the third light, the voice of your heart's desire, turn green.

Just as God put a desire in Nehemiah's heart, He put a desire in my heart and in Kim's heart to start the church in St. Louis. The green light of the third signal assured us that the action we were about to take was in line with God's plan and timing in bringing our bigger heart's desire, our vision, to pass.

## THE VOICE OF YOUR CIRCUMSTANCES

**God Confirms the Plan.**

When following God, we aren't led by circumstances. "(For we walk by faith, not by sight:)" (2 Cor. 5:7 KJV). Instead, we're led by the Holy

Spirit. We follow the inward peace that comes from listening to His voice. Sometimes, we will see an opportunity presented in a circumstance, but we know to consult the Holy Spirit and follow the other signals to be sure it's from God, not something that will sidetrack us. When Kim and I were looking for a bass boat, the circumstance of seeing one for sale and the owner even coming down on the price didn't mean that God wanted us to buy that boat!

God often uses the fourth signal, the voice of your circumstances, to encourage you along the way. When we already know in our spirit that we are going the way God has for us and the other traffic signals are green, God will cause things to happen to confirm to us that we are going in the right direction. These circumstances occur after we are sure we are about to take the correct step. They don't happen as "signs" beforehand to help us make the decision. We don't follow signs; we follow the Holy Spirit. "Signs" occur to encourage us after we've made the decision.

God may confirm in a way that delights us! But He wants us to rejoice in Him no matter where we are and what we see going on around us. So the first part of Psalm 37:4 tells us to delight ourselves in the Lord: "Delight yourself also in the Lord, and He shall give you the desires of your heart."

Philippians 4:4 tells us, "Rejoice in the Lord always: and again I say, Rejoice" (KJV). Paul wrote Philippians when he was in prison! When we are in circumstances that contradict the type of life we know God has for us, we are to rejoice. We walk by faith in Him and His Word, not by what we see happening in our lives. So we keep walking and applying what we are to do, rejoicing in knowing He is for us and taking us to the excellent place He has for us.

Instead of being unhappy with where we are, we need to trust what God is doing, obey what He is giving us to do in that step and rejoice in Him. God wants us to do our part by delighting in where we are and busying ourselves, being fully productive, and continuing to take action as doers of the Word. (James 1:22 KJV.) He wants us to do everything He has for us with all our hearts (Col. 3:23 NIV) to prepare us for the next step. Then, when we do our part, He can do His part, often in a miraculous way, to take us there.

Some people look around, murmur, complain, gripe, or get mad at God and everybody else. We don't want to let a voice of our circumstances from the enemy stop us from moving forward into our destiny. Each of us has a choice to let circumstances make or break us, to be better or bitter, to be a victim or victor. We need to have a mindset of rejoicing in the midst of seemingly negative circumstances to stay open to hearing from God. Then, when we remain obedient and rejoice in the step where we are, we often see God respond quickly.

*Each of us has a choice to let circumstances make or break us, to be better or bitter, to be a victim or victor.*

A couple in my church told me, "We prayed and feel God wants us to relocate and move. But we have a house and car to sell and many other things to do quickly. What in the world are we going to do?" I felt led by the Holy Spirit to tell them, "Just be faithful with this step, then I think it will be a domino effect: all the other steps will fall into place like dominoes."

Within a week, their house sold; the next week, their car sold—everything was supernaturally expedited. They had taken the first step and obeyed God. That's a powerful demonstration of the results brought by rejoicing in what we know the Lord is doing and immediately taking the steps of obedience He gives us. We can slow down our progress by wasting time complaining and not trusting God.

God is preparing our next step into the future. If we don't complete what He has for us in our current situation, we may be delayed in taking that step, or unprepared when we get there.

God's ways and thoughts are higher than ours (Isa. 55:9 KJV), and His plans for us are better than ours. Max Lucado said, "What Christ does in us and through us will always be 'exceedingly abundantly above all we ask or think.'" God wants to give us our heart's desire and sometimes even more.

We may not, and many times won't, see or understand what God is doing. Although the circumstances may appear to be the opposite of what we're expecting, we know to rejoice and do everything we have to do with all our hearts! God is leading us and working for us no matter where we are in His process.

When we delight ourselves in Him in every step and continue obeying Him in every way, we will see He will tell us the next step at the right time. He wants us to fully experience life where we are as we walk in each step He has for us.

Whether the decisions we need to make are major or minor, God wants us to succeed in walking in His will. He doesn't want us to be confused or live in a state of chaos. Instead, He wants us to be in the right place at the right time, using the right method, and He wants our lives to be full of His peace, joy, and confidence.

David said, "May He grant you according to your heart's desire, and fulfill all your purpose" (Ps. 20:4). So let God put His desire in your heart and bring it to pass.

God is for you. He wants to fulfill your heart's desire in every area and make all your plans succeed, so rejoice!

# 9

# YOUR FUTURE IS GOOD

## Flourish

I f you're not good with numbers and don't like math, algebra, or details, then more than likely, God isn't calling you to be an accountant!

## THE VOICE OF YOUR GIFTS AND STRENGTHS

**What are you naturally good at doing?**

The fifth way to identify God's call on your life is by looking at your giftings—gifts, talents, abilities, and strengths—that God gave you. As touched on in a previous chapter, your calling will match your gifts. In the plan God has for you to pursue, what you're doing will feel natural and flow easily.

> *Jesus gives us the ability to bear good fruit.*

For example, at our church, I noticed someone producing a video who is a natural at it—has a natural bent for it. This person has the gift of communication. The gifts match the calling.

When we're using our gifts to live in our purpose, we'll feel satisfied knowing we're doing what we're supposed to be doing in life. Our talents and our calling enable us to be fruitful. It's rewarding to see good fruit result from the joy of using our gifts to fulfill the calling God has for us. Remember, there are souls attached to our gifts and calling. Someday in the future, people will thank you because you used your God-given talent.

Jesus gives us the ability to bear good fruit: "Abide in Me, and I in you. As the branch cannot bear fruit of itself, unless it abides in the vine, neither can you, unless you abide in Me" (John 15:4). So we who abide in Jesus and He in us bear much fruit. (v. 5.)

John 15:7-8 continues: "If you abide in Me, and My words abide in you, you will ask what you desire, and it shall be done for you. By this My Father is glorified, that you bear much fruit; so you will be My disciples."

These verses remind us to keep dwelling on God's Word so that it abides in us, in our thinking. Our desires will line up with God's desires, and He will bring our heart's desire to pass. And we will bear much fruit, which will glorify Him. Don't be in such a rush to get to another season that you miss what God wants you to learn about yourself here and now. If you pick the blossom, you must do without the fruit.

When the Holy Spirit lives in us, His fruit is in us. It's available in us to affect the way we are and the way we live. Galatians 5:22 describes "the fruit of the Spirit" as "the result of His presence within us" (AMP). Verses 22-23 tell us that the fruit of the Spirit is ". . . love [unselfish concern for others], joy, [inner] peace, patience [not the ability to wait, but how we act while waiting], kindness, goodness, faithfulness, gentleness, self-control . . ." (AMP).

As we are changed into becoming more like Jesus by focusing on the Word and thinking in line with it, the fruit of the Spirit is more apparent in us. We allow Jesus to show through in our nature and everything we do. We are able to display the fruit in areas we have struggled with, patience, for example. As we use our gifts to fulfill our calling, actions—our Holy Spirit-guided good works—are the good fruit we produce.

Some people don't know their gifts, especially their spiritual ones. At Church on the Rock, we help our people identify their giftings. We guide them in growing spiritually and, in that process, give them a test to discover their spiritual gift. Identifying that gift leads them to their calling and learning God's will for their life. The responsibilities in that calling are characteristic of that gift and flow naturally. And the results that follow from using their talents in their calling are so remarkable that people comment in amazement over what the Lord has done.

When we're in the right fit, we flow and flourish. But if we get out of our lane or out of our call, we won't have peace about what we're doing and may veer off onto rough roads or into a ditch.

But remember, we all have a calling; it comes with gifts, and, as discussed in previous chapters, God never withdraws the gifts. ". . . the gifts and the calling of God are irrevocable" (Rom. 11:29). God doesn't change His mind about the gifts He gives, to whom He gives them, and whom He calls. We can always change our direction to get back on the right road. If you veered off, learn from the experience and return to the right course!

At the fifth traffic signal, the voice of your gifts and strengths, ask yourself whether the skills, talents, and abilities God gave you complement the calling you identify as God's plan for you. Does it center on what you're good at doing? If yes, the light is green, which signals a powerful and significant confirmation that you are moving in the direction God created for you.

Sometimes you, or other people, think you should pursue a particular field or area, but your aptitudes are specifically suited to something else, which will reveal itself as God's plan for you. Occasionally God leads us into an unfamiliar area where we do things we are not particularly good at to stretch us, cause us to learn new things, and trust Him more. But in fulfilling our life purpose, we use the gifts and strengths God has given us to succeed and excel for Him in all we do.

*His dream for our lives is an uncommon life that glorifies Him.*

If people, usually well-meaning, even those close to you who you know want the best for you, give you advice to go into a field that doesn't fit with your gifts, check the traffic signals, and don't pursue it if the Holy Spirit isn't giving you peace! John C. Maxwell says, "Do not take the agenda that someone else has mapped out for your life."

There's a pull to get us to settle for less, be common, conform, be and do like everyone else. But nothing could be further from God's plan for us. His dream for our lives is an uncommon life that glorifies Him.

Be yourself. "No one ever made a difference being like everybody else" (P. T. Barnum).

However, we do need godly counsel and advice! The Bible tells us, "... in a multitude of counselors there is safety" (Prov. 24:6). But we need to be very careful about who we consult.

## THE VOICE OF SEASONED LEADERS

**Consult leaders who have been successful in what you want to do.**

When Kim and I came to St. Louis to plant Church on the Rock, I talked to people who had successfully done what we wanted to do. I asked two or three seasoned leaders, who were church planters and highly respected ministers, who I knew also respected me, for their advice. I asked, "What types of things did you go through to establish your church?" "What were your biggest problems and greatest challenges?" Of course, we can learn from our mistakes or from hearing about other people's mistakes. But, of course, it's better to learn from other people's mistakes!

Elders are people who are mature in life and experienced in following God in faith. We need to consult elders we know who are doing what we want to do and who know us. We need to ask advice from leaders who love us, believe in us and our calling, are for us, want to help us, and will tell us the truth. We want to consult them, but even so, we don't necessarily have to act on what they tell us. We profit from their advice whether we directly apply it to our plans or use it to improve our approach and, in both cases, to avoid pitfalls. But we still follow the other traffic signals and the step-by-step specific plan God is showing us.

Before asking any person for advice, ask people you respect who to go to for advice. If a leader doesn't have a track record of success in doing what you're interested in, don't ask for the person's advice! Never discuss your problem with someone who is incapable of contributing to the solution. And never share your dream with unproductive people. Talking to someone who hasn't been in the area you're considering or didn't excel in the way you want to succeed in it won't help produce the kind of overwhelmingly victorious results you're expecting. As we saw in previous chapters, when you know how big the God who is for you is, you know He wants to do big things through your ministry and in every area of your life as you fulfill your purpose.

In the earlier days of Church on the Rock, when 1,000 to 1,500 were attending, I consulted Dr. Roy H. Hicks, a seasoned minister with a track record of starting successful churches, for advice on who to consult. I asked him, "Who's the greatest pastor in America? Who is the person with the greatest pastor's heart?" He said, "Hands down, John Osteen."

## GOD IS FOR YOU

John Osteen founded and pastored Lakewood Church in Houston, Texas, now pastored by his son, Joel Osteen. Many leaders I would have liked to talk with weren't easy to meet because their ministries were so big; if they didn't know you, scheduling an appointment would have been difficult. So I mentored with them through their books and their audio messages. I bought all of John Osteen's audio messages and books and became very familiar with his teaching. But nobody except for God knew my heart's desire was to be personally mentored by John Osteen.

Sometimes God uses our godly associations, our friends, to arrange divine appointments. For example, one day a minister friend called and asked if I would like to go with him the next day to a meeting in Houston with some other ministers, including John Osteen. So the next day, we flew to Houston and went to the restaurant where they were meeting. Ministers with megachurches were sitting around the table, one of whom was John Osteen.

The ministers were telling John about their churches, ministry, and books. I was sitting there listening. After a while, John looked at me and said, "You're not saying anything." I said, "I didn't come here to hear me talk; I came here to hear you talk." That statement opened the door. I filled a notepad with what he said.

I went home and told Kim, "I want to be mentored by John Osteen. I want him to be my pastor."

I called his assistant. After I explained the connection through my friend who John knew and that I had met John, I told her with great passion, "I'd like to come down and ask him some questions sometime."

She said, "Okay," and scheduled an appointment! So I took my notes and flew into Houston for one day, rented a car, and went to Lakewood Church. Meeting with a ministry leader of that size was new to me. It seemed as though everything was on a grand scale. There was a guard and a large lobby. I went to John's office, and his assistant took me in to sit down and meet with him.

After we exchanged hellos, I started asking him the questions I had written on my yellow pad.

When I finished, he said, "Is that all you've got?"

I said, "Pastor Osteen, I have one more question. Would you be my pastor? Would you mentor me?"

He said, "No. I can't do that. I'm too busy. Honestly, I have seven thousand pastors right now who look to me as their pastor. They call me their pastor. I don't have time for another one. Sorry."

I said, "Well, please pray for me and lay hands on me. Release your anointing."

I knelt down; he put his hands on me and prayed over me.

I said, "Thank you," and left.

The next day I was working in my office, and my assistant told me Pastor Osteen's assistant was on the phone for me. His assistant put me through to John, who said, "Dave, did you really mean what you said yesterday? Do you want me to be your pastor?" I said, "Yes." He said, "I'll do it."

He was very serious about being my pastor. Every month he sent videos to our church. Every month I called him, and if I hadn't called for some reason, he would inquire as to why. I went to Houston to meet with him regularly.

God uses elders who are friends to encourage us and emphasize how much He is for us and our future, as he did with Hilton Sutton when he told me he wished I would begin to see myself as God sees me and the plan that He has for my life and future.

God used John Osteen to encourage me even in our last conversation. I was on my treadmill at home when the phone rang. I answered.

A little voice on the other end said, "Dave." It was John.

I said, "Pastor! Yes."

He said, "You're my Elisha. I'm your Elijah. Don't get discouraged."

I said, "I'm not."

He said, "Run your race and finish your course."

He died the next day.

In the Bible, we read that before Elijah the prophet was taken to heaven, he and Elisha, his successor (1 Kings 19:16 NIV), had the following discussion: ". . . Elijah said to Elisha, 'Ask! What may I do for you, before I am taken away from you?' Elisha said, 'Please let a double portion of your spirit be upon me'" (2 Kings 2:9).

I understood John's encouraging words to mean I should unswervingly press forward in applying all I had learned from him, and I would succeed, as he had through God, in the ministry and purpose God had for me.

> To become who you want to be in the future, develop the habits of the person you want to become.

This is an example of how God works in our lives when we follow His signals to walk into the future He has for us. God fulfilled my heart's desire, His desire, with the particular seasoned leader I had wanted to mentor me in how to succeed in a similar type of ministry. And following John's advice has produced much fruit in my life and ministry.

## BEGIN BECOMING THE PERSON IN YOUR FUTURE, TODAY

As we're following the signals that move us in the direction God has for us, we need to do the things today that will take us to the destination. We need to intentionally build daily habits that will bring the result.

Our daily habits and processes are more important than the finished product, fulfilling our destiny because they take us there. The results are a by-product of the process, and the results take care of themselves.

Bill Walsh, winner of three Super Bowl championships as head coach of the San Francisco 49ers, broadcaster, and author of *The Score Takes Care of Itself: My Philosophy of Leadership*, said, "Concentrate on what will produce results rather than on the results, the process rather than the prize."

To become who you want to be in the future, develop the habits of the person you want to become. Look at the patterns of the leaders who are highly successful in doing what you want to do, and follow their examples.

In the early days of Church on the Rock, I wanted to know the habits of pastors who had churches like the future church Kim and I knew we wanted.

I studied the habits of John Osteen and other highly successful pastors. I visited their churches, and God gave me favor and arranged ways to form relationships with many of them. I learned what I needed to do to become who I needed to be to pastor a church like theirs.

I developed habits similar to theirs and made them my routine. I asked God to search me, as we read in Psalm 139:23-24 that David did. I wanted God to show me any habits and attitudes I needed to change that were holding me back. I gave up some things and sacrificed some things to pay the price each day to reach my future. But every price has a prize.

The secret to your success is hidden in your daily routine. I've discovered this good news: God-directed habits, once established, can be as hard to break as bad habits.

What you're doing today won't show up today, but it will show up in the future. And this same principle applies in every area of life. What you do today is important. Even though you start small, you will see big results. The Bible tells us, "Do not despise these small beginnings, for the Lord rejoices to see the work begin . . ." (Zech. 4:10 NLT). This verse refers to the big result of Zerubbabel building the temple in Jerusalem! "Zerubbabel is the one who laid the foundation of this Temple, and he will complete it . . ." (v. 9 NLT).

Pursue the vision your gifts support. Develop your gifts and strengths to fulfill your calling, and let Jesus live through you to bear much good fruit. Study the habits of the leaders who have succeeded in what you want to do, and begin building similar habits in your daily routine. Remember, God is bigger than your past. Focus on who you are becoming, not what you've lost or your past mistakes.

Charles H. Spurgeon said, "When you stand before men, ask little, and expect less; but when you stand before God, ask much, and expect more, and believe that he is able to do for you exceeding abundantly above all that you ask or think."

Find out what you need to do today to build the kind of future you want, the future God has for you, and start doing it. You may start small, but you will see big results. Expect the big God who is for you to do great things!

# 10

# YOUR FUTURE IS GOOD

## When Your Faith Is in God

It takes faith to do God's will. When Kim and I started Church on the Rock, we left a denominational church where we were pastors. We had insurance and a retirement plan. We were safe, secure, and stable.

Like Abram (later to become "Abraham," Gen. 17:5) in the Bible, who followed God's instructions to go to "a land that I will show you" (Gen. 12:1), we went to plant the church not knowing exactly what was ahead. We were going where we had no income, financial support, insurance, equipment, or building, and we were planning to have our church meet in a library and hotel. In addition, we had no idea how many people would come to the services.

Our parents thought we were crazy, and I understand why. They said, "What are you doing?" We took their grandkids, Daniel and Stephen to come, and left in November of 1983, right before the holidays.

We were a young couple. I was thirty years old, and Kim was twenty-eight. Kim was pregnant with Stephen. Our son, Daniel, was a little guy. But we had God; we had seen Him work before in our lives, and we were so excited to be moving out in the plan He had for us.

## THE VOICE OF FAITH

**Step out in obedience to God, believing He will bring the vision to pass.**

We had the green light on the first six traffic lights. We were in line with the Word and had the peace of God. We were following our heart's desire, God's desire, to start the church. God had confirmed our plan; we had some experience and knew we were operating in our gifts and strengths. We also had God's counsel through seasoned leaders experienced in starting exceptionally successful churches. Now we were at the seventh traffic light. It takes the voice of faith to step out of your comfort zone and go where you've never been to do what you've never done in obedience to God.

How did Kim and I do that? How could we leave a place of security to move into a new life with so many unknowns?

From a natural standpoint, the situation looked impossible, illogical, and, as our parents thought, crazy. It didn't make sense. Why would we leave a great church we were pastoring with an excellent salary, benefits, and reputation, and on a pathway to an even better ministry and life?

Why? We knew it was God's will for us, and we had to be in God's perfect will. We agreed with what Smith Wigglesworth said, "If you seek nothing but the will of God, He will always put you in the right place at the right time."

We had faith in God and His promises. We knew by following Him, we would see His will for us come to pass. We had belief that He is a rewarder. "... without faith it is impossible to please Him, for he who comes to God must believe that He is, and that He is a rewarder of those who diligently seek Him" (Heb. 11:6).

Kim and I were filled with joy, peace, and hope in believing. Romans 15:13 tells us, "Now may the God of hope fill you with all joy and peace in believing, that you may abound in hope by the power of the Holy Spirit."

To do what God called you to do, you need faith that He will bring it to pass. When you take that step to do what you feel God is calling you to in that job, career, business deal, marriage, corporation, or decision, you'll experience joy, continue in peace, and be full of hope. The seventh traffic signal, the voice of faith, will be green.

*To do what God called you to do, you need faith that He will bring it to pass.*

It took faith to start our Church on the Rock with an attendance of thirty-five (a few but wonderful) people at our first service and no insurance, money, or building. It took faith in God, His will, and His promises. It takes faith to walk in the will of God every day. And it takes faith to keep pressing through to the finish no matter what happens. "Let God's promises shine on your problems," says Corrie ten Boom.

## LIFE IS NOT ALWAYS FAIR, BUT GOD IS ALWAYS FAITHFUL

When we were starting our brand-new church in St. Louis, our son Stephen was born prematurely. It was a cesarean delivery and a dire situation. The doctors told us he wasn't supposed to live! In fact, a doctor came to me and said, "Don't worry about naming him right now; he's not going to make it."

Stephen was rushed to a children's hospital. Kim was in the other hospital recovering from the surgery. Our first son, Daniel, was with a babysitter.

I will never forget that dismal, rainy day. Stephen was 100 percent dependent on a respirator to breathe. He was in an incubator. The doctors said he wasn't going to make it. Because we had left our secure position and location, not only did we not have insurance, much money, or a church building, we didn't have support from a close group of family and friends nearby. It was the loneliest I've ever felt in my life. I thought, *I just wish I had somebody to go through this with me.*

Then Kim called me from the hospital and said God had spoken to her to lay hands on the baby, and the baby would recover. "Go down and pray for him now, and lay hands on him. God's going to work a miracle."

I went to the hospital and prayed for Stephen. And God answered with a miracle! Within twenty-four hours, Stephen was off the respirator. The nurses began referring to him as "the miracle baby." And within a couple of weeks, Stephen was home! God's faithfulness turned the terrible situation around into good. He brought us overwhelming victory! I share this miraculous story with you because, as Max Anders says, "Every demonstration of God's faithfulness to us is an opportunity for us to testify of Him to others."

## YOU CAN COUNT ON GOD'S FAITHFULNESS

Don't let anything stop you from doing what you know God wants you to do. Although many things around you may change and you may face enormous challenges, as Kim and I did, God never changes, and He is faithful. You can trust Him to come through with the victory. Malachi 3:6 says, ". . . I am the Lord, I change not . . ." (KJV), and Lamentations 3:22-23 tells us, "The faithful love of the Lord never ends! His mercies never cease. Great is his faithfulness . . ." (NLT). Stay faithful. God isn't finished with you yet.

God never alters the vision He gives us. He never gives up on it or takes it back. "He who calls you is faithful, who also will do it" (1 Thess. 5:24). He is for us and wants to partner with us to finish our course with excellence. He wants to turn our difficult circumstances into something beautiful for us and His purpose.

Especially in the highs and lows we go through, the turbulent times, we need to concentrate on looking at God's faithfulness. This simply means focusing on His character and His promises. Understanding God's character takes us through crises. We know we can count on Him to fulfill His promises in our lives. God is at His best when our circumstances are at their worst.

## GOD IS FAITHFUL TO DO THE IMPOSSIBLE

God made Abram a promise that looked impossible to fulfill. Abram and his wife, Sarai (later "Sarah," Gen. 17:15), were childless and too old to have children. (Heb. 11:11-12.) But God told Abram that He would make him "a great nation"; he and Sarai would have a son, and she would be "a mother of nations." (Gen. 12:2; Gen. 17:16.) "... the Lord made a covenant with Abram, saying: 'To your descendants I have given this land...'" (Gen. 15:18). This was "... all the land of Canaan..." (Gen. 17:8).

Hebrews 11:11 says Sarai "was past the age" to bear children, and because of Abram's age, the Bible describes him "... as good as dead..." (v. 12)! When God first told Abram to go to "... a land that I will show you. I will make you a great nation," "... Abram was seventy-five years old..." (Gen. 12:1-2, 4). God assured Abram that "one who will come from your own body shall be your heir" (Gen. 15:4), and Abram's descendants would be as numerous as the stars. (v. 5.) Abram "... believed in the Lord, and He accounted it to him for righteousness" (v. 6). Abram believed in God's faithfulness.

It was a very long time before God brought the promise of Abram and Sarai having a son to pass. Twenty-five years after God had first told Abram he would be a great nation, He provided more details: "When Abram was ninety-nine years old, the Lord appeared to Abram and said, '... I will make My covenant between Me and you, and will multiply you exceedingly'"

(Gen. 17:1-2). ". . . Sarah your wife shall bear you a son, and you shall call his name Isaac . . ." (v. 19). ". . . My covenant I will establish with Isaac, whom Sarah shall bear to you at this set time next year" (v. 21).

The Lord ". . . visited Sarah as He had said . . ." (Gen. 21:1)! "The Lord kept his word and did for Sarah exactly what he had promised. She became pregnant, and she gave birth to a son for Abraham in his old age. This happened at just the time God had said it would. And Abraham named their son Isaac" (Gen. 21:1-3 NLT).

When Isaac was born, Abraham was "one hundred years old" and Sarah was "ninety years old" (Gen. 17:17). It took faith for Abram and Sarai to believe and obey God to receive the promise! They had faith in God's faithfulness from focusing on His character and promises.

*God can handle any impossibility, including whatever you're facing right now.*

Regardless of the circumstances (Rom. 4:19), Abraham pressed through in the belief that God would do what He said. He kept believing until he saw the promise fulfilled. Abraham ". . . did not waver at the promise of God through unbelief, but was strengthened in faith, giving glory to God, and being fully convinced that what He had promised He was also able to perform" (vv. 20-22).

There were times when both Abram and Sarai looked at the impossibility of the situation. In fact, separately, each laughed at the idea! (Gen. 17:17; 18:10-12.) But they changed their focus from the circumstances to look at God's great faithfulness. God can handle any impossibility, including whatever you're facing right now.

What made the difference that caused Sarah to conceive and have the baby, Isaac? How did it happen? What was the missing ingredient, the turning point, the tipping point, the revelation that took her from the impossible to the possible, from weakness to strength? What did she do that changed everything?

Hebrews 11:11 gives us the answer. "By faith Sarah herself also received strength to conceive seed, and she bore a child when she was past the age, because she judged Him faithful who had promised."

When Sarah received a revelation of the character of God—He is faithful and will bring to pass what He has promised—she conceived.

Has God ever given you a promise that looks impossible for Him to bring to pass as He did with Abram and Sarai? He may have given you a promise that looks even more unlikely now than when He first told you, possibly years before. Every day, focus on God's character and promises—on who He is and what He has said in His Word. God is a good, big, great, and faithful God who does what He says He will do.

Don't waiver; don't give up—God keeps His promises. Trust God with your tomorrows because He was faithful yesterday.

## WE CAN TRUST GOD

When people promise us something, we want to know who they are and what their character is like to decide whether we can trust them to do what they say. In the same way, we need to know who God is, His character—His attributes as we saw in Psalm 139—to understand that He is completely trustworthy to do what He has promised. We need to know that we can build our lives on His faithfulness. "What God has for you, is for you. Trust His timing. Trust His plan" (Unknown).

We've all gone through times when people we know, even people close to us, didn't keep their word. When Kim and I were in college, a pastor I admired made us a promise. We were anticipating and looking forward to the result. But a few weeks before the time he had said he would do it, he called and broke his promise.

This man who had been an example and a role model to me, who I thought was faithful, didn't do what he had said he would. I felt very hurt and taken aback. His unfaithfulness jarred me. It took me a little while to work through that experience emotionally. But Kim and I proceeded full force ahead, and God moved in many other ways to take us into the abundance of living our vision despite the unfaithfulness of a person!

*God is the same on our good days and bad days.*

We shouldn't expect people around us to be perfect. And we know that we shouldn't expect ourselves to be perfect, either. As faithful as we try to be, we will still fail. But even when we falter, God is faithful. "If we are unfaithful, he remains faithful, for he cannot deny who he is" (2 Tim. 2:13 NLT). God is faithful in loving us even when we've gone completely off course, whether unintentionally or intentionally. To bring us back to moving forward with Him, He will continue working behind the scenes to show us His love and that He is for us. He did this with me after the tremendous loss of my brother, Rick. Never give up on God because He never gives up on you!

People will fail us, including ourselves. We may experience terrible circumstances—an apparently hopeless situation, as the doctors said Kim and I were facing with Stephen. We may have lost loved ones, a job, or a business. But we need to take our eyes off our disappointment in the unfaithfulness of people and the negative circumstances to instead focus on God's faithfulness.

God is the same on our good days and bad days. When we fail, we keep serving Him no matter what by focusing on who He is and what He said He would do. Charles Spurgeon said, "The glory of God's faithfulness is that no sin of ours has ever made him unfaithful."

## HOPE IN GOD

The prophet Jeremiah understood God's faithfulness and focused on it in the midst of destruction. He and his people had gone through incredible hardship. In fact, it was an adverse set of circumstances the people brought on themselves.

Jeremiah called out to God's people with warnings from God to repent and change their ungodly practices, or destroyers would bring devastation to Jerusalem. (Jer. 22:6-9 contains one of those passages.) Jeremiah cried out to them for years, but the people ignored his words. As a result, the Babylonians invaded and brought tremendous destruction to the city, including the temple and the people.

In anguish over the terrible desolation, brokenness, murder, and rape, Jeremiah said, "I will never forget this awful time, as I grieve over my loss" (Lam. 3:20 NLT). But despite the circumstances—the desperate, horrific time of hurt, heartache, and death—Jeremiah was the person quoted earlier in this chapter who praised God for His great faithfulness. "Yet I still dare to hope when I remember this: The faithful love of the Lord never ends! His mercies never cease. Great is his faithfulness; his mercies begin afresh each morning. I say to myself, 'The Lord is my inheritance; therefore, I will hope in him!'" (vv. 21-24 NLT).

Another translation of verse 24 states, "'The Lord is my portion . . .'" Psalm 16:5 explains the meaning of "The Lord is the portion of my inheritance . . ." (AMP) as ". . . my cup of blessing. You guard all that is mine" (NLT).

Despite the grief, Jeremiah turned and looked at God's faithfulness, which brought hope and faith. He intentionally changed his focus from looking at the devastation to thinking about who God is. Lamentations 3:21 NLT says, "Yet I still dare to hope when I remember this"; words this verse, "This I recall to my mind; therefore I have hope." When you know God's promises are true you find hope during challenging times.

To Jeremiah, it brought hope "when I remember," "I recall," thoughts about God's faithful love, never-ending mercies, and faithfulness. (vv. 22-23.) This was Jeremiah's cup of blessing, and God guarding all that was his.

Hope starts in your thinking, your thought process. Everything begins with a thought. Proverbs 23:7 tells us, "For as he thinks in his heart, so is he . . ." So to have hope, change the way you think.

Instead of dwelling on past hurts or mistakes—a hang-up, habit; the news; the unfaithfulness of a Christian brother, sister, family member, or someone else who disappointed you; a bad experience—replace those thoughts by recalling what the Word says about God's character and promises.

## WE CAN WAIT FOR THE PROMISE BECAUSE WE HAVE HOPE

Jeremiah refers to waiting in connection with hope. "The Lord is good to those who wait for Him, to the soul who seeks Him. It is good that one should hope and wait quietly for the salvation of the Lord" (Lam. 3:25-26).

It is crucial to know that the Bible discusses hoping and waiting together, because without hope, we won't wait. And as we know, sometimes we don't see any evidence that God has been working for us in the natural world around us for quite a while. But we know to have faith that He is. So we need to wait to experience what He has been preparing behind the scenes. We need hope to wait upon Him, and hope comes from focusing on the faithfulness of God.

As Abraham waited for years to see God fulfill the promise He had made him, Abraham remembered God's faithfulness; he kept God's promise before him by thinking about it and hoping. "Even when there was no reason for hope, Abraham kept hoping—believing that he would become the father of many nations. For God had said to him, 'That's how many descendants you will have!'" (Rom. 4:18 NLT). So Abraham believed in God's faithfulness and hoped and waited for God to bring the promise to pass. And as we know, God did! God may take longer than you think to deliver His promises, but He never breaks them. That you can be sure of!

## FEED ON GOD'S FAITHFULNESS

We learn from Hebrews 3:16-18 that the children of Israel who disobeyed God didn't enter the promised land because of unbelief. They didn't receive the promise. We also know that "...faith comes by hearing, and hearing by the word of God" (Rom. 10:17).

Sometimes people, who don't understand God's trustworthiness because they haven't renewed their minds to the Word about His faithfulness and dependability to do what the Bible says He will do, try to apply one of His promises in their lives, but waiver. Then, when they face difficulties or circumstances that appear to block them from moving forward toward fulfilling their calling, they give up. They don't understand how much God is for them and is faithfully, relentlessly working on their behalf even when the opposite appears to happen. They don't have a revelation that if they persevere, they will see God bring an exceedingly victorious outcome.

They need to feed on who the Word says God is, persevere, and see His result in their lives and in the lives of the people they influence.

Psalm 37:3 tells us, "Trust (lean on, rely on, and be confident) in the Lord and do good; so shall you dwell in the land and feed surely on His faithfulness, and truly you shall be fed" AMPC). The *Holy Bible, New Living Translation* says, ". . . Then you will live safely in the land and prosper." One translation words the phrase "feed surely on His faithfulness" as "cultivate faithfulness" (NASB). Be confident in the Lord and do good, which means in this verse, do what He says, live well in the land, and feed on His faithfulness.

Feed on God's faithfulness through meditating on the Scripture verses about God's character, who God is, and His faithfulness to bring His promises to pass. Then, memorize, personalize, and visualize them.

For example, Psalm 36:5 says, "Your mercy, O Lord, is in the heavens; Your faithfulness reaches to the clouds."

Another passage to feed on that we discussed in a previous chapter concerning our heart's desires is Psalm 37:5: "Commit your way to the Lord [roll and repose each care of your load on Him]; trust (lean on, rely on, and be confident) also in Him and He will bring it to pass" (AMPC).

And focus on the verses with God's promises. For example:

3 John 1:2: "Beloved, I pray that you may prosper in all things and be in health, just as your soul prospers."

2 Corinthians 2:14: "Now thanks be to God who always leads us in triumph in Christ, and through us diffuses the fragrance of His knowledge in every place."

Philippians 4:19: "But my God shall supply all your need according to his riches in glory by Christ Jesus" (KJV).

1 Peter 2:24: ". . . Himself bore our sins in His own body on the tree, that we, having died to sins, might live for righteousness—by whose stripes you were healed."

Psalm 34:19: "Many are the afflictions of the righteous, but the Lord delivers him out of them all."

Because the things we focus on get bigger, keep your thoughts on what you know to be true about God's character and promises. Magnify His faithfulness. Journal about it. Apply it—let Him show you how faithful He is. Declare His faithfulness. Speak about it. Say He is faithful in your family, finances, and health—your life and future. And say, "God said it in His Word, so that settles it; I'm going to say it until I see the promise come to pass."

Hebrews 10:23 assures us, "Let us hold fast the profession of our faith without wavering; (for he is faithful that promised;)" (KJV). So, likewise, the

*New King James Version* says, "Let us hold fast the confession of our hope without wavering . . ."

When you build your faith and confidence in God by feeding on the Word, and you obey Him, there is a benefit: ". . . you shall be fed" (Ps. 37:3 AMPC). You will be nourished, strengthened, and refreshed. You'll reframe the way you think, so you're thinking the right thoughts. What looked impossible will be possible because you'll know God will do what He promised. He will bring it to pass. We know how all this ends. You win. God wins.

*To finish strong, focus on God's faithfulness.*

As we build trust in God as faithful, we will run to Him in times of trouble. And the more revelation we have of God's faithfulness, the more we can trust Him to do bigger things. Our Church on the Rock is already ministering to far more people than Kim and I originally imagined. To finish strong, focus on God's faithfulness.

When you're making a decision, large or small, when you're wondering specifically what you should do with your life, career, job, business, or ministry—whether you should marry the person you're dating, what car or house you should buy, where you should send your kids to school, or what exactly to do in any situation you encounter during the day—you know how to hear the specific answers God has for you. So when the first six traffic signals are green, listen to the voice of faith, and let the joy, peace, and hope in believing flood you as you take that step into the exciting, fulfilling, and productive future God has for you! God is faithful. God has never stopped being good. And He never will.

# 11

# YOUR FUTURE IS GOOD

## Favor, Family, Friends, and Opportunities

God has an abundance of benefits and blessings available for us that many of us never receive. There is so much the God who is for you wants to give you and use to impact the world around you!

Years ago, before Kim and I started Church on the Rock, I bought a new car I thought was awesome. It was cool, and I was so excited about it. I had it for a couple of years. Then I went to trade it in for a different car.

The salesperson looked at it and started listing all the options it had. There were many, but I wasn't aware of any of them! I had driven the car for all that time, and although I thought it was incredible, I hadn't been enjoying it in the way I could have if I had known all its features and how to use them! I hadn't looked at the instruction manual even once.

God's Word is the instruction manual that shows us all the benefits, options, and blessings that God intends for us to receive and how to apply them to our lives intentionally. Learn what they are and use them. Let God fulfill all the good He has planned for you!

## FAVOR BRINGS OPPORTUNITIES

God's favor is one of those benefits many Christ followers don't know is available to them. We saw in previous chapters that it is one of the ways God shows He is for us. He brings us opportunities and gives us favor with people to move us forward in ways we couldn't have imagined!

*If we're looking at our limitations, we'll miss our opportunities.*

Expect God's favor and opportunity to come. Watch for it, then act. The people who act on the opportunities God opens up for them through favor are the ones who fulfill their God-given dreams and purpose on the planet, the reason that they're here. On the other side of obedience is an open door.

Some people think other people get the good breaks because they were raised in an affluent home with all the advantages. But, as people of God, no matter our status or background, we need to expect that God will send us the right people at the right place at the right time with the right opportunity for the right outcome. These are the people we need who will help us fulfill what we were put on earth to do.

The enemy will try to get us to look at our limitations: what we don't have, can't do, where we are, who isn't helping us, and who let us down and disappointed us. If we're looking at our limitations, we'll miss our opportunities. We'll miss the people God wants us to form friendships with and the place we should be. "One touch of His [God's] favor can put you fifty years ahead of where you thought you'd be" (Joel Osteen).

People with a victim mentality, who focus on other people's advantages, may dwell on the past and feel sorry for themselves. Because of the economy, they may have lost their jobs, careers, retirement, or funds or aren't as wealthy or well-off as they used to be. These are enormous challenges. But people who focus only on the obstacles, no matter how big and time-consuming, and dwell on thoughts such as getting older, no longer feeling as capable as they once were, and concluding their time is over won't live with an attitude of expecting to see the doors of opportunity God opens. Or they may see them but won't take advantage of the situations God arranges because they've been too busy focusing on the negative. At Church on the Rock, during rough times in the country, we've seen some people facing overwhelming obstacles become millionaires!

## BLESSING AND FAVOR

Blessing and favor are connected. Psalm 5:12 tells us, "For You, O Lord, will bless the righteous; with favor You will surround him as with a shield."

God sees those of us who believe in Jesus as righteous. Jesus, who knew no sin became sin for us, ". . . that we might become the righteousness of God in Him" (2 Cor. 5:21). Another version states, ". . . in Him we would become the righteousness of God [that is, we would be made acceptable to Him and placed in a right relationship with Him by His gracious lovingkindness]" (AMP). When we believe in Jesus, we become the righteousness of God, meaning we are in the right relationship with Him, and God blesses the righteous with favor!

We also have the blessing of Abram (Abraham) as his spiritual descendant. We are among his descendants about whom God told Abram would be as numerous as the stars. (Gen 15:5 AMP.) Galatians 3 tells us, ". . . if you are Christ's, then you are Abraham's seed, and heirs according to the promise" (v. 29) and that for believers in Jesus, ". . . the blessing of Abraham might come upon the Gentiles in Christ Jesus, that we might receive the promise of the Spirit through faith" (v. 14).

God told Abram, "I will make you a great nation; I will bless you . . . and you shall be a blessing . . . and in you all the families of the earth shall be blessed" (Gen. 12:2-3). And Abram was prosperous in physical possessions as well. "Abram was very rich in livestock, in silver, and in gold" (Gen. 13:2).

*Our friends frame our world.*

We who are believers in Jesus have blessings and favor available to us. Favor brings us opportunities, and acting on them brings blessing that flows with more blessings. Do your best; God will do the rest. So daily, we should get our eyes off potential obstacles and look for the opportunities God wants to use to bless us.

We can miss the moment of favor that God has planned for our promotion not only by looking at the obstacles instead of the opportunities but by having the wrong associations in our lives. Choose your friends carefully.

## FRIENDS INFLUENCE OUR FUTURE

Our friends frame our world. They have a significant influence on determining our future. They contribute to our fruitfulness and effectiveness in fulfilling our callings, and we contribute to theirs. A best friend always brings out the best in you. Ecclesiastes 4:9 tells us, "Two people are better off than one, for they can help each other succeed" (NLT).

We need to evaluate which friends are building us up, strengthening, and encouraging us, and if any are bringing us down, causing us to be distracted from where God wants us to go and what He wants us to do. We minister to people in all kinds of situations, but to be effective in moving forward, we must be selective about the close friendships we form. We don't want relationships that are draining or dysfunctional. Friends help determine the direction of our lives.

Let God guide you in choosing your relationships. People who are attracted to a group of other people they can never get in with may be tempted to become upset with God or the people in the group. The people feeling rejected may start looking down on themselves and feed or develop a poor self-image. But they need to realize that all the time, God wants to direct their paths to keep them from associating with the wrong people for themselves. Good people may be in the group, but they won't take the ones feeling left out in the direction they need to go. God wants to take us to the right people to keep us moving forward on the course He has for us.

Proverbs 27:17 says, "As iron sharpens iron, so a friend sharpens a friend" (NLT). Another wording of Proverbs 27:17 is, "Iron sharpens iron; so a man sharpens the countenance of his friend [to show rage or worthy purpose]" (AMPC). The way our countenance appears, our eyes and face—whether we're smiling or frowning—reflects our attitude, approach, and appearance—whether we're bitter or getting better. Do our friends bring out the worst—rage and anger? Or the very best—a worthy purpose?

First Corinthians 15:33 tells us, "Do not be deceived: 'Bad company corrupts good morals'" (AMP). Because I had friends that were a bad influence when I was growing up, I was going in the wrong and potentially devastating direction until my pastor stood up for me in court after I was arrested and set me on a different path. Relationships and friendships can make or break us. Unfortunately, some parents don't realize their children's peers are a more powerful influence than they are. The wrong associations in your life can take you down the wrong path.

Good friendships are God's idea, and they are critical. Good friends sharpen us into pursuing our worthy purpose. In choosing our friends, we need to be selective to be effective. God is for good relationships. Make friends before you need them.

The proper order in forming relationships is spiritual first, then physical. Therefore, it is crucial when dating for the priorities to be spiritual before emotional, then physical. We all have different circles, or levels, of friends, some closer and more intimate, but all should be founded on spiritual similarities centering around Jesus first.

There is a third individual in a relationship besides you and the other person who makes it strong, enduring, overcoming, fulfilling, and thrilling. "And though a man might prevail against him who is alone, two will withstand him. A threefold cord is not quickly broken" (Eccl. 4:12 AMPC). The three-fold cord is you, the other person, and Christ in the center of the relationship.

The Bible gives us more advice about choosing friends. First, look at how you will walk together. "Can two walk together, except they be agreed?" (Amos 3:3 KJV). Do the person's philosophy, values, and spiritual beliefs agree with yours? What is the person's character like? Does the person have integrity? Before you become entangled emotionally, follow the Word's advice. For example, Proverbs 22:24-25 tells us, "Make no friendship with an angry man, and with a furious man do not go, lest you learn his ways and set a snare for your soul."

You're created for connection. God didn't write solo parts for any of us. We can pick up the ways of our friends and become like them. As my friends are, I will become. "He who walks with wise men will be wise, but the companion of fools will be destroyed" (Prov. 13:20).

Just as following the steps God gives us through the seven traffic signals and forming good relationships will take us to the right place at the right time, developing bad relationships will take us to the wrong place at the wrong time. We can miss our destiny by associating with the wrong people. Look at our friends, and we'll know our future. Relationships contribute to our achievements in life. This is why the order of priority is spiritual, emotional, and last, physical.

> *If we want the right friends, we need to be the type of friend we want.*

To bring to pass His overall plan, a major purpose God has in using relationships formed for spiritual reasons is to combine the individual goals of those in the body of Christ who are applying their particular gifts to fulfill their callings. (1 Cor. 12:12; Rom. 12:4-5.) He uses relationships to bless the current generation and to pass down what He wants to do to the next generation.

Esteem the relationships God directs you to form. Evaluate the ones you have, and realize you might need to eliminate some. Disconnect from them so you can develop the ones God wants by expanding them. In friendships, we need to evaluate them, esteem the good ones, and eliminate the ones that aren't in line with our values and what God wants us to have and nurture. Expect God's favor in them.

We've all invested in, poured into, and mentored people who turned around and hurt us. After an experience like that, we may have thought, *I will never do that again. It just doesn't pay off.* But what you put into other people does pay off with other good friendships. Ecclesiastes 11:1 tells us, "Cast your bread upon the waters, for you will find it after many days."

The God relationships, the God connections, are those that God ordained for your life. Concentrate on expanding them by nurturing, feeding, and making deposits in them. Invest, impart, encourage, refresh, and edify the people in your relationships. Build them up, and believe in them. Sow good seeds into their lives.

If we want the right friends, we need to be the type of friend we want. In John 15:12, we read the definition of friendship when Jesus said, "This is My commandment, that you love one another as I have loved you." He also said, "You are My friends if you do whatever I command you" (v. 14). He said again, "These things I command you, that you love one another" (v. 17).

## EXPECT GOD'S FAVOR AND OPPORTUNITIES

As in the example of John Osteen, I became friends with leaders who affected my future with their advice, example, connections, and ministry, whom I would never have met if it hadn't been for God's favor.

# GOD IS FOR YOU

Marilyn Hickey is a Bible teacher well-known for her ministry in both America and overseas. Marilyn and her husband, Wallace (Wally), founded Happy Church, now Encounter Church, in Colorado. Marilyn is the type of seasoned leader I wanted to consult when Kim and I were pursuing God's will at the sixth traffic signal. I wanted to meet her.

I called her office and ordered every audio teaching she had. I told the person who answered the phone, "I want everything." Later that day, someone at her ministry called me and said, "Marilyn Hickey wants to talk to you"!

Around 150 people attended our church then. Because she saw I valued her wisdom, she gave me her time. She started coming to see us every year. She and Kim talk every week.

## GOD CAN RESTORE MISSED OPPORTUNITIES

The doors of opportunity are marked "push." So, acting on an opportunity when we have one is important. But if we miss an open door that God provided for us, we know that, like other mistakes we've made, God can turn it around for good. But in His mercy, He may also arrange for us to have the opportunity we missed come back to us again!

Jerry Savelle is another leader, minister, and author I know. I was in Fort Worth, Texas, attending a conference with his board when Jerry's pilot walked up to me. He said, "Dave, I'm going to California to pick up Oral. He's tomorrow's speaker. Come and jump on the plane with me. If you would like to go, it will be just you, Oral, and me in the jet." This was Oral Roberts.

Kim and I were also going to take care of some things with Daniel, who was in college there. I said, "I'm sorry. I can't do it." He was surprised. I explained, "No, I have obligations." So I didn't do it. It would have been an opportunity to glean from Oral Roberts and his experience, from California to Texas in a private jet! I regretted that decision every time I thought about it.

So one day, I told Marilyn, "I missed an opportunity to meet one-on-one with Oral Roberts. Could you ever make that happen?" She said, "I'll make it happen," and she did.

Oral Roberts was still living in California, and when Kim and I were on our way to a conference in Hawaii, Marilyn made it happen.

With three or four other pastors, Kim and I went to Oral Roberts's house and sat down with him. He talked with all of us. We asked questions, and he answered them. I asked him, "Before we go, would you lay hands on Kim and me and pray over us?"

We knelt, and he prayed. That was the beginning of an amazing and rewarding relationship with him. He wrote Kim and me handwritten notes after that until he passed away.

In the area of our heart's desires, God will arrange relationships and friendships—connections—that contribute to us fulfilling our destiny and future.

We must do what we need to do for God to pour all He wants to do into our lives. We saw this with Naaman following the instructions of Elisha through his messenger to wash in the river Jordan seven times to be healed of leprosy.

I ordered all of Marilyn's teachings because I admired what she was doing and wanted to learn from her, not because I was trying to get in favor with her through an ulterior motive. When I placed the order, God had a connection for me I didn't know about in advance. My action allowed God to move on my behalf to give me favor with her. And because we formed a relationship, I was able to ask her if it would be possible for her to arrange a way for me to meet with Oral Roberts.

Other friends have opened the door for me to meet other seasoned and highly successful leaders who became friends and were influential in Kim and me fulfilling our calling. But as we saw in previous chapters, we must do our part to allow God to continue moving us forward. Remember that Charlie "Tremendous" Jones said, "You will be the same person in five years as you are today except for the people you meet and the books you read."

## YOUR PART AND GOD'S PART

We do our part so that God can do His part. And we need to cooperate with God even when we don't see the reason for what He is telling us to do or the end result at the time. We must follow Him and obey as Abram did when God told Him to go to "a land that I will show you" (Gen. 12:1). Hebrews 11:8 tells us, "By faith Abraham obeyed when he was called to go out to the place which he would receive as an inheritance. And he went out, not knowing where he was going."

*Just because God has a future planned for us doesn't mean it will happen. Therefore, we need to do our part through obedience to clear the way for God to do His part to bring our vision to pass.*

When God told Abram to leave his country and go to a land He would show him, Abram didn't know where he was going and why, but he immediately obeyed. And eventually, God revealed the details of His plan. Kim and I followed this example when we left where we were to start Church on the Rock. As a result, we are fulfilling our calling in a way that exceeds anything we could have imagined!

Just because God has a future planned for us doesn't mean it will happen. Therefore, we need to do our part through obedience to clear the way for God to do His part to bring our vision to pass.

John 2:1-10 tells of a wedding in Cana of Galilee when the wine ran out. Mary, Jesus's mother, told Jesus there was no wine and told the servants to do whatever Jesus instructed. Jesus said to fill six waterpots with water and draw some out for the master of the feast to taste. The master of the feast responded by telling the bridegroom, ". . . Every man at the beginning sets out the good wine, and when the guests have well drunk, then the inferior. You have kept the good wine until now!" (v. 10).

Jesus turned the water into wine, and it was exceptional wine, far above the quality the master of the feast expected. Jesus did His part, but Mary and the servants first did their part by following His instructions. And Jesus brought to pass the result in an even greater way than anyone anticipated, just as He does for us when we submit to Him and follow His instructions. As we know, God will ". . . do exceedingly abundantly above all that we ask or think . . ." (Eph. 3:20).

We're blessed when we do what the Word says and obey God. We see in the Old Testament that there was a premise, a condition, to meet for every promise. For example, Deuteronomy 28:1-14 describes the premise and blessings for the children of Israel. The premise is in verse 1: "Now it shall come to pass, if you diligently obey the voice of the Lord your God, to observe carefully all His commandments which I command you today . . .", then verses 2-14 list the tremendous blessings that will result from their obedience. There has always been a part we are to do. God will do His part when we do our part.

God will carry out His Word in our life when we partner with Him. Deuteronomy 7:9 says, "Therefore know that the Lord your God, He is God, the faithful God who keeps covenant and mercy for a thousand generations with those who love Him and keep His commandments."

God wants to be a partner in our labor. And, if God is your partner—make your plans big. Don't frustrate yourself with shallow water. To succeed beyond your wildest dreams, you have to have some wild dreams. He is working with us, and we are working with Him. It takes cooperation to fulfill God's will in our lives.

God brought the children of Israel out of Egypt, where they had been enslaved, to bring them into the promised land. (Exod. 1:1-14; Exod. 6:2-8; Exod. 14.) He brought them out to bring them in, but He didn't bring them in because they didn't cooperate with Him. The awesome God wanted to be a partner in their labor. For Him to bring the promise to pass, He wanted them to be co-laborers with Him. Instead, they murmured, complained, griped, were ungrateful, and otherwise expressed their unhappiness. (Deut. 1:6-8, 10-11, 20-21, 26.) They wanted to go back to Egypt! (Num. 14:1-4.) So because they didn't participate, the adults except for Caleb, to whom God would give the land on which he walked because he wholly followed Him (Deut. 1:35-36), and Joshua, who would cause Israel to inherit the land (Deut. 1:38), died in the wilderness. (Num. 14:29-32.)

Even though it was God's will for the Israelites to enter the promised land, God's will didn't come to pass because the children of Israel didn't do their part. They didn't cooperate with Him. They hadn't done their part for God to do His part.

Favor comes through opportunities, open doors, relationships, timing, positioning, preparation, wisdom, revelation, and other ways. We need to have a mindset of having God's favor in our lives and do our part to act when we see God's opportunities and the people He has arranged for us to meet. Favor produces excellent victories in the midst of great impossibilities.

Expect God's favor. Surrender to His instructions, and do your part. Obey what He tells you to do. And let Him bless you immeasurably!

# 12

# GOD IS FOR YOUR SECURITY

## Finances

Our greatest security today is not in our abilities, careers, or assets; it's in the covenant, the blessing of Abraham, that is ours as spiritual descendants of Abraham through Jesus. The blessings described in Deuteronomy 28:2-14 show us in detail the type of security God provides through the covenant. For example, verse 6 tells us that we will be blessed wherever we go and in whatever we do. (NLT.) The Lord will cause our enemies who rise up against us to be defeated (v. 7), and He will give us great prosperity. (v. 11 AMP.) Verse 2 tells us all these blessings will come upon and overtake us!

A covenant is a contract, an agreement. In our covenant, we have benefits, rights, and privileges as children of the Most High God. A covenant also has terms. We need to fulfill the terms of our covenant by doing our part for God to do His part, as we have seen. We know that our part is following and obeying God so that He can take us where we need to go to fulfill His plan.

# GOD IS FOR YOU

> *Not only does God give His people the power to get wealth so that He may establish His covenant, He also teaches them how to profit.*

God expects us to use our minds and reason! But many times it's God's plan for us to follow Him without seeing how our actions will bring a logical result. As we saw in previous chapters, some acts of obedience won't make sense to our natural minds because God's ways and thoughts are higher than ours. (Isa. 55:9.) Remember, "...lean not on your own understanding..." (Prov. 3:5). When we're following God in obedience to Him and His Word and we think, *Doing that doesn't make sense!*, we need to go ahead and do it. And what is God's response? He turns the circumstance into a miracle and brings a supernatural supply!

## GOD IS FOR OUR FINANCIAL SECURITY

Part of God's covenant with His people includes financial security. In addressing Israel, Moses said, "And you shall remember the Lord your God, for it is He who gives you power to get wealth, that He may establish His covenant which He swore to your fathers, as it is this day" (Deut. 8:18).

Not only does God give His people the power to get wealth so that He may establish His covenant, He also teaches them how to profit: "Thus says the Lord, your Redeemer, the Holy One of Israel: 'I am the Lord your God, who teaches you to profit, who leads you by the way you should go'" (Isa. 48:17).

Even in times of layoffs, slumps, recessions, depressions, or famines, God will prosper us. In the midst of famine, Isaac was blessed because he obeyed God. Originally, Isaac planned to go to Egypt to escape the famine. Doing that would have been logical according to the world's system of prospering and the right action to take if God hadn't intervened with another plan. Instead, God instructed Isaac to live in the land He directed and reminded him of his covenant with Him through his father, Abraham. (Gen. 26:1-5.)

This was the land of famine! And because Isaac obeyed, God blessed him there. God told Isaac, "... Do not go down to Egypt; live in the land of which I shall tell you. Dwell in this land, and I will be with you and bless you ... I will perform the oath which I swore to Abraham your father" (vv. 2-3). Sometimes God tells us to stop instead of go. In Isaac's case, God stopped him from following the world's system to remind him to depend on Him and His covenant. Personally, when God has told me, "Stop," obeying His voice has saved me a great deal of money, heartache, time, and energy.

Isaac did His part in fulfilling the terms of the covenant by obeying God and staying in the land as God told him, and God did His part. "Then Isaac sowed in that land, and reaped in the same year a hundredfold; and the Lord blessed him. The man began to prosper, and continued prospering until he became very prosperous" (Gen. 26:12-13). Sometimes the God who is for us works in the most unexpected ways and places to bring about the desired result!

## IN THE RIGHT PLACE DOING THE RIGHT THING

Isaac was a farmer. He understood agriculture, and he went to work. He was diligent at what he did best. He was sowing seed into the ground in a famine, and God blessed and prospered him!

Obey God by following the Holy Spirit to be where you're supposed to be, doing what you're supposed to be doing. And whatever skill, talent, ability, or craft you're best at that you identified at the fifth traffic signal, keep getting better at it. Notice that Deuteronomy 8:18 doesn't say God gives us wealth; it tells us He gives us the "power to get wealth." The ability to get wealth comes through applying our unique gifts and strengths that God gave us to fulfill our purpose.

In the midst of a downturn, your reputation will spread and be known. When other people are being let go, you'll be kept on. Your employer won't want to lose you and won't be able to afford to let you go because you're doing what you do best and are valuable to the company. You've developed your craft and skill, and are diligent in a time of famine and recession. Everything else around you may be on hold or in a lull, but you're prospering. Things around you may be depressed and receding, but you're proceeding. God will keep making room for us to prosper.

## GOD'S PURPOSE IN PROSPERING HIS PEOPLE

> God's purpose in prospering His people and increasing our wealth is to carry out the Great Commission.

David said, "'Let the Lord be magnified, who has pleasure in the prosperity of His servant'" (Ps. 35:27). God wants us to have enough to take care of our children and to help our parents, to help the needy and poor, support our local church, and leave an inheritance for the next generations. (Prov. 13:22.)

He wants His people to live an abundantly good life, but not for the purpose of buying everything we want. He wants to bless us with things; He isn't against us having things we want, like the bass fishing boat I wanted for our family outings. In fact, He delighted in guiding me so that we would have a top-of-the-line kind rather than the used one I originally looked at. God wants us to have good things but doesn't want them to become a priority to us. Money itself is not evil; it's the love of it: ". . . the love of money is a root of all kinds of evil . . ." (1 Tim. 6:10).

God's purpose in prospering His people and increasing our wealth is to carry out the Great Commission: "And Jesus came and spoke to them, saying, 'All authority has been given to Me in heaven and on earth. Go therefore and make disciples of all the nations, baptizing them in the name of the Father and of the Son and of the Holy Spirit, teaching them to observe all things that I have commanded you; and lo, I am with you always, even to the end of the age.' Amen" (Matt. 28:18-20).

Fulfilling our calling is part of God's plan in carrying out His overall purpose: spreading the message of Jesus throughout the world and establishing His covenant on the earth. God wants us to have money to evangelize the world. And as we walk out our part of God's greater vision, we are blessed in many ways, including financially. When believers know the purpose of prosperity, they won't worship it.

We need to keep our trust not ". . . in uncertain riches but in the living God, who gives us richly all things to enjoy" (1 Tim. 6:17). We are to trust not in the uncertain world system—the stock market, our portfolio, or our employer, but in the God who is for our finances and shows us how to profit, who tells us when to go and stop and puts us in a position where we can use our skills to succeed. God wants us to keep our focus on Him and ". . . be rich in good works, ready to give, willing to share" (v. 18), keeping as a priority going out into the world to look for people who are hurting and have needs, or who have a common interest, to reach out and relate to them with His love.

We need money to fulfill God's purpose for our lives. Some people need more than others because God's plans for them require large amounts of financial resources. The money we're blessed with isn't actually money: it's people—souls and precious lives. The more money all of us make, the more we can give to God's work to spread the message of Jesus and the good God intends for all people.

Matthew 6 tells us, "Do not lay up for yourselves treasures on earth, where moth and rust destroy and where thieves break in and steal; but lay up for yourselves treasures in heaven, where neither moth nor rust destroys and where thieves do not break in and steal" (vv. 19-20). By using our treasures on earth to finance the gospel, we are laying up treasures of born-again people, souls, in heaven.

## GOD'S PLAN FOR FINANCIAL SECURITY

As we have seen, God is for us financially. And Malachi 3:8-12 shows us tithing is God's plan to prosper His people. Verse 10 identifies "the tithes" as "the tenth" (AMP). Our tithe is the foundation for the success of our finances. It is 10 percent of our income, and it protects the remaining 90 percent.

Verse 10 also describes the way God uses tithing to bless us. "'Bring all the tithes into the storehouse, that there may be food in My house, and try Me now in this,' says the Lord of hosts, 'if I will not open for you the windows of heaven and pour out for you such blessing that there will not be room enough to receive it.'"

This doesn't mean that God will literally open a window in the skies and pour money out of it when you tithe. He opens the windows of heaven over you by pouring out favor on your life. God will work in many ways to bless everything your hand touches with such favor that the result is overwhelming.

## PREFERENTIAL TREATMENT

One way God uses the blessing of favor poured out from heaven for our financial good is through preferential treatment. If you are a believer in Jesus and haven't experienced that happening, start looking for God's favor and opportunities. Favor can change policies, rules, and regulations to your advantage. And favor produces recognition even when you seem the least likely to receive it.

Years ago, Kim and I were going back for a third year of college in Texas but didn't have the money to pay for it. We had student loans and didn't want to take out any more loans. Still, we went ahead with the process of enrolling.

I was standing in the office to register, believing God would meet our financial need, and in my mind giving Him all the glory that He would do it. I walked up to the desk and went through all the classes I wanted with the person registering me.

She said, "How are you going to pay?"

I said, "I've taken out student loans and don't want to take out any more loans. I've been working at the college full time, forty hours a week, and carrying a full-time load at school. I really don't know."

She said, "Wait just a second." She walked over to another office and after a minute came back.

She said, "Come with me," and took me to the registrar. He said we could go to the third year for free! A sponsored program paid our tuition.

We were doing our part to follow the Holy Spirit to be in college. We worked to make money, always tithed, and enrolled. Did it make sense to the natural mind to consistently tithe when we didn't have the money for tuition? No, but James 1:22 says, ". . . be doers of the word . . ." We were living according to God's ways, and He opened the windows of heaven and poured out a blessing of favor that gave us an open door that supplied our tuition! It's important to always be Spirit-led and align ourselves with God and His Word to let Him do His part to provide for us financially and in every other way.

## OUR BEST

We learn from the Word to give God the first of our income, our best, our firstfruits, not the leftovers after we pay our bills. Proverbs 3:9-10 describes the results of giving our firstfruits (our best): "Honor the Lord with your wealth and with the first fruits of all your crops (income); then your barns will be abundantly filled and your vats will overflow with new wine" (AMP). When we give God our best, He will provide abundantly for us!

Moses told the Israelites to give God their best, their firstfruits. He instructed the Israelites that when they had come into the land God had given them as an inheritance, possessed it, and dwelled in it (Deut. 26:1), ". . . you shall take some of the first of all the produce of the ground, which you shall bring from your land that the Lord your God is giving you . . ." (v. 2). This was the blessed land ". . . flowing with milk and honey . . ." (v. 9) that God had promised Abraham in the covenant He would give them.

Moses also told the Israelites where to give their firstfruits: ". . . go to the place where the Lord your God chooses to make His name abide" (Deut. 26:2). Another version words verse 2 as, ". . . the designated place of worship—the place the Lord your God chooses for his name to be honored" (NLT). We won't find His name lifted up and honored over a theme park or bar. God wants us to enjoy good things in life, such as taking our family on vacation to a theme park, and He wants us to give to worthy causes and good works, but our firstfruits go to the place God's name is honored, where the name of Jesus is preached and exalted, our local church.

*When we tithe, not only does God pour abundant blessing from heaven on our lives, He, "the Lord of hosts," will also, "'. . . rebuke the devourer for your sakes."*

In the place God chose, the Israelites were to give their first produce to the priest (Deut. 26:2-4), and Genesis 14 tells us that Abram gave "a tithe" (v. 20) to the priest. "Melchizedek . . . was the priest of God Most High" (Gen. 14:18), ". . . and Abram gave him a tenth of all . . ." (v. 20 AMP). Hebrews 4:14 tells us, ". . . we have a great High Priest . . . Jesus the Son of God." The priest Melchizedek is a representation to us, a type and shadow, of our High Priest Jesus Christ. When we give to our local church, we are giving, not to man, but to our High Priest, Jesus. God uses our firstfruits and tithes to support our local church.

GIVE GOD THE OPPORTUNITY TO BLESS YOU

When we tithe, not only does God pour abundant blessing from heaven on our lives, He, "the Lord of hosts," will also, "'. . . rebuke the devourer for your sakes, so that he will not destroy the fruit of your ground, nor shall the vine fail to bear fruit for you in the field . . .'" (Mal. 3:11). God rebukes the devourer from our finances, and our money goes further. We have fewer medical bills and accidents. Our vehicles and appliances, washers and dryers run longer.

Malachi 3:10 discusses tithes. Tithes are different from offerings. The tithe comes off the top of our income, and any amounts we give beyond the tithe are classified as offerings.

God doesn't need our money. He has gates of pearls and a street of gold. (Rev. 21:21.) He is ". . . God Most High, Possessor of heaven and earth" (Gen 14:19). He owns everything: "The earth is the Lord's, and everything in it . . ." (Ps. 24:1 NLT). However, Malachi 3 tells us there is a way to rob God! "Will a man rob God? Yet you have robbed Me! But you say, 'In what way have we robbed You?' In tithes and offerings" (v. 8).

Not giving tithes and offerings is robbing God! But if He owns everything, what are we robbing from Him? We're robbing God of the opportunity to bless us in the many ways He desires because He is good.

## RESCUED FROM THE CURSE

Malachi 3:9 says, "You are cursed with a curse, for you have robbed Me, even this whole nation." Just as Deuteronomy 28:2-14 describes the blessings that result from obeying the voice of the Lord God and doing His commandments (vv. 1-2), Deuteronomy 28:15-68 describes the curses that result from not obeying the voice of God and observing His commandments. (v. 15).

However, Galatians 3:13 tells us, "Christ has redeemed us from the curse of the law, having become a curse for us (for it is written, 'Cursed is everyone who hangs on a tree')" with the result we saw in a previous chapter, "that the blessing of Abraham might come upon the Gentiles in Christ Jesus . . . through faith" (v. 14). When we believe in Jesus, we are redeemed from the curse! Or as another version words verse 13, "... Christ has rescued us from the curse pronounced by the law..." (NLT).

Although Jesus has redeemed us from the curse, obedience is still important in the New Testament, the new covenant, as we know. Obedience was important in the Old Testament, and it is important in the New Testament but in a different way.

In the Old Testament, the underlying instruction of Deuteronomy 28 was to obey God's voice and observe His commandments. In the New Testament, we are also instructed to obey God's voice and do what His Word says, but we live by Jesus's statement, "This is My commandment, that you love one another as I have loved you" (John 15:12). "For by grace you have been saved through faith, and that not of yourselves; it is the gift of God, not of works, lest anyone should boast" (Eph. 2:8-9). We are saved by faith in Jesus (Rom. 10:9-10), not by our works.

We intentionally live in obedience to God and His Word as an expression of our love for God. And from our position of right relationship with God through Jesus, we obey and do good works.

God wants us to obey so that we will be in the right place at the right time to see His plan for us come to pass! Keep walking in obedience: tithe and give offerings. And get ready for God to pour out favor and blessings on your life too abundant to receive!

# 13

# GOD IS FOR YOUR SECURITY
## FOCUS ON HIM

When we're walking in obedience to the Lord, we need to remember we're not perfect—we're pursuing! God is looking for hearts that are hungry for Him. When we completely fail or miss what we were supposed to do, we repent, get up, come back to Him, and go on.

And we need to keep trusting that God is bringing His overall plan to pass. In the passage below, we see the Israelites were looking at the wicked who were prospering instead of looking at God and His promises.

God told the Israelites their words had been harsh against Him (Mal. 3:13) because they said, ". . . It is useless to serve God; what profit is it that we have kept His ordinance, and that we have walked as mourners before the Lord of hosts?" (v. 14), and ". . . those who do wickedness are raised up; they even tempt God and go free . . ." (v. 15).

# GOD IS FOR YOU

Psalm 73 shows a similar instance when Asaph the psalmist was complaining. But then he changed his perspective. "... I saw the prosperity of the wicked" (v. 3 KJV) "until I went into the sanctuary of God; then I understood their end" (v. 17).

## LOOK AT THE BIG PICTURE

In the sanctuary, God gave Asaph the big picture. Of the wicked, Asaph wrote, "Oh, how they are brought to desolation, as in a moment! ..." (v. 19). "For indeed, those who are far from You shall perish..." (v. 27).

Follow the example of Asaph who concluded, "... I have put my trust in the Lord God, that I may declare all Your works" (v. 28). Moses instructed the Israelites (Deut. 26) after they gave their firstfruits to the priest and he had set them down before the altar, that they were to acknowledge what the Lord had done to bring them out of slavery into the promised land and worship Him. (vv. 2-10.) Then they were to "... rejoice in every good thing which the Lord your God has given to you and your house, you and the Levite and the stranger who is among you" (v. 11).

*It's time for us to stop tolerating lack financially and in every other area.*

Guard against speaking harsh words against the Lord about the wicked who are prospering. Instead, look at Him and keep your eyes on the big picture. Trust in Him and rejoice! Speak words in faith over your tithes and offerings in line with His Word and desire for you to prosper.

When we obey and give our tithes and offerings, the devourer is rebuked for our sake, but the devil will try to bring fear. When we are about to give and he comes with the thought, *Don't do that! You could pay one of your bills with that money. You won't have enough*, we know what to do.

Don't accept the devil's lie. Take the thought into captivity, and replace it with the truth that agrees with the Word.

We need to be assertive and aggressive, not against people, but against the devil's attempts to keep us from receiving the benefits and blessings God has for us, the abundance of good in our life that is available to us in Jesus. It's time for us to stop tolerating lack financially and in every other area. We need to take our stand in our dominion and the authority Jesus gave us to receive what belongs to us.

## FOCUS ON GOD AND HIS PROMISES

Use your authority to possess your possessions, your benefits in Jesus, or you may not receive them. Keep speaking the Word aloud in faith over your offering! Hebrews 10:23 tells us, "Let us hold fast the confession of our hope without wavering, for He who promised is faithful." Proverbs 18:21says, "Death and life are in the power of the tongue . . ."

Personalize the promises by applying them to you, your family, those you are praying for, and situations. Say, "I'm a tither. The devourer is rebuked for my sake. I'm blessed!" (Mal. 3:10-11.) Declare aloud the blessings of Deuteronomy 28:2-14 over yourself and your family. Say, "Let the Lord be magnified, who has pleasure in the prosperity of His servant" (Ps. 35:27). "The Lord has pleasure in the prosperity of my family and me!" "According to Isaiah 54:17, no weapon formed against me shall prosper." "God is for me; who can be against me?" (Rom. 8:31.)

Speak, don't doubt in your heart, believe what you're saying will be done, and you will have what you're saying. (Mark 11:23.) The name of Jesus is powerful. All authority has been given to Jesus. (Matt. 28:18.) And whatever we ask (in line with God's will) in His name, He will do, that the Father may be glorified in Him. (John 14:13.) Remind the devil that, in Jesus's name, he is defeated (1 John 3:8; Col. 1:13; Heb. 2:14), and He who is in you is greater than he (the devil) who is in the world. (1 John 4:4.)

# GOD IS FOR YOU

If the devil is trying to wreck your marriage, don't stand for it. Use the authority God made available to you through Jesus. "Therefore submit to God. Resist the devil and he will flee from you" (James 4:7). Again, submit and obey for God to take action in the way He desires in your life to bless and protect you. We must walk in obedience to God in line with His Word for His authority to work.

*By speaking in agreement with God's will that we know from His Word, we set His power in motion that will cause change.*

By speaking in agreement with God's will that we know from His Word, we set His power in motion that will cause change. We can change our marriage, family, relationships, financial status, or ministry.

We saw in Psalm 103:2-5 that one of God's benefits is the healing of all our diseases. (v. 3.) First Peter 2:24 tells us that Jesus not only took on our sins, He provided healing for us: ". . . Himself bore our sins in His own body on the tree, that we, having died to sins, might live for righteousness—by whose stripes you were healed." With our God-given authority, we can set God's power in motion to change a negative diagnosis!

The day you take dominion over your marriage, kids, health, or other circumstance is the day of turnaround. You set the turnaround in motion in the spiritual realm, then you will see it come to pass in the natural realm. Say, "My marriage is blessed in every area! My kids will not be on drugs! They will not be dope addicts or alcoholics. My daughters will not get pregnant before they're married. My kids will not be a part of illicit sex! No sickness or disease will attack my family! In Jesus's name!" Keep speaking and believing until you see the result. Have faith that you will see it happen!

# GOD IS FOR YOUR SECURITY | FOCUS ON HIM

Don't waver. When we get under pressure, we want to speak in line with what we feel, what we see, and what we're going through. Don't do that! People who are doubting and wavering say, "I wish I hadn't tithed. I wish I hadn't given that amount in the offering. What if I'm laid off? We'll lose the car and house. I was better off living the world's way!" Just as the Israelites had done, they are saying it's useless to serve God instead of focusing on His promises and faithfulness.

## THE BLESSING OF GIVING

When we give, we're sowing seeds. We give to the poor and to help people. And with our other offerings, it is important to plan and be very strategic in giving so that the good our seeds do multiplies. When we give to givers, doers, people who are blessing other people and making a difference for God in the world—good stewards of their finances—the seed will multiply through God guiding them and using what they're doing. Our seed will continue to multiply through their lives. This is planting our seed in good ground. There are different types of ground.

When we give to stingy people, tightwads, and small thinkers who can't hold down a job because they won't make an effort to apply themselves or learn what they need to know to succeed, we are planting our seed in poor ground. Stingy people will stop the multiplication of that seed because the seed sown will not multiply through their lives.

Plant in good ground by giving to those who have. They will use the seed well.

We give out of compassion and love because we want others to know God is for them and we want them to receive all He has for them through Jesus. But when we give, God also blesses us.

As we saw in a previous chapter, Ecclesiastes 11:1 tells us, "Cast your bread upon the waters, for you will find it after many days." The tide that takes your offering out will bring your generosity back to you. Another translation words this verse, "Send your grain across the seas, and in time, profits will flow back to you" (NLT). Even if we plant a seed in the life of someone or something else where the seed is unlikely to grow and produce in that kind of soil, God will still bless our giving in our lives.

Sowing and reaping is a principle that operates in every area of life. The Bible tells us, "But this I say: He who sows sparingly will also reap sparingly, and he who sows bountifully will also reap bountifully" (2 Cor. 9:6).

When Kim and I had our first son, Daniel, who was still a baby, we were youth pastors in a great church at Iowa State University in Ames. However, we were having a hard time because we barely made enough money to get by. The church had set us up as self-employed, which meant we paid the taxes ourselves that employers of directly hired employees would withhold from their paychecks.

It was almost time for us to pay our taxes, but we didn't have the money. One weekend we gathered up all the loose change we had accumulated over several months in old jars and gave it to the youth group, where I was teaching on giving. We spread out the change among everyone there. We needed a miracle.

A couple of weeks later, someone in the church said to Kim and me, "Come out to our car after the service." When we did, he opened his trunk to show us the coin collection he had kept up all his life. He said, "We just felt led to give this to you."

Kim and I had sowed coins, and we reaped his coin collection! He had no idea we had planted a seed of coins. I took the collection to a dealer in downtown Ames who bought it for the exact amount we needed to pay our taxes! We bountifully sowed all the coins we had and trusted God, and we reaped bountifully. God performed a financial miracle!

We are to purpose in our hearts to give with the right motive and attitude. Second Corinthians 9 continues with verse 7: "So let each one give as he purposes in his heart, not grudgingly or of necessity; for God loves a cheerful giver," ". . . [whose heart is in his giving]" (v. 7 AMPC).

Luke 6:38 tells us, "Give, and it will be given to you: good measure, pressed down, shaken together, and running over will be put into your bosom. For with the same measure that you use, it will be measured back to you."

Some people give with a wrong motive and attitude. Instead of giving to bless others so ". . . that blessings may come to someone . . ." (2 Cor. 9:6 AMPC), they give from a selfish motive. They think Luke 6:38 means that God is some kind of spiritual slot machine and giving tithes and offerings causes Him to pay off with automatic blessings. Their motive in giving is to receive money to spend on themselves, not because they want to bless others for God. James 4:3 says, "You ask and do not receive, because you ask amiss, that you may spend it on your pleasures."

*Faith isn't a formula. Faith is trust, based on a relationship with God that's rooted in love.*

God isn't like a slot machine. He doesn't work that way! Faith isn't a formula. Faith is trust, based on a relationship with God that's rooted in love. Galatians 6:7-8 tells us, "Do not be deceived, God is not mocked; for whatever a man sows, that he will also reap. For he who sows to his flesh will of the flesh reap corruption, but he who sows to the Spirit will of the Spirit reap everlasting life."

". . . only faith activated and energized and expressed and working through love" is what ". . . counts for anything . . ." (Gal. 5:6 AMPC.) The right motive is giving out of love.

## GOD IS OUR STANDARD, NOT THE WORLD

Again, living according to God's system financially doesn't make sense to people living according to the world's system. We are giving and living according to God's standards. The world isn't our standard—God is.

Doing what Luke 6:38 tells us doesn't make sense to the world. Luke 6:27-28 also tell us, ". . . Love your enemies, do good to those who hate you, bless those who curse you, and pray for those who spitefully use you." "And just as you want men to do to you, you also do to them likewise" (v. 31). ". . . be merciful . . . judge not . . . condemn not, and you shall not be condemned. Forgive, and you will be forgiven" (vv. 36-37).

Again, to ". . . love your enemies, do good, and lend, hoping for nothing in return . . ." (v. 35) doesn't make sense to the world. This is not the way the world acts, as Luke 6:32-34 makes clear: "...if you love those who love you, what credit is that to you? For even sinners love those who love them" (v. 32), do good to those who do good to them, and lend to receive back. (vv. 33-34.)

Luke 6:35 continues and tells us, as we know, there is a reward for obeying God: ". . . Then your reward from heaven will be very great, and you will truly be acting as children of the Most High, for he is kind to those who are unthankful and wicked" (NLT). "Therefore be merciful, just as your Father also is merciful" (v. 36).

## LOOK AT GOD'S PROMISES

We live according to God's multiplication standards, not the world's methods. Instead of being a slave to the culture or situations around us, we are to look ". . . at the things which are not seen . . ." (2 Cor. 4:18), the things we know God is doing based on His promises in the Word. Ecclesiastes 11:6 tells us to consistently sow. "In the morning sow your seed, and in the evening do not withhold your hand; for you do not know which will prosper, either this or that, or whether both alike will be good."

People who are looking for perfect conditions to give never will. They are letting their circumstances and emotions dictate their actions. Ecclesiastes 11:4 describes this inaction: "He who observes the wind will not sow, and he who regards the clouds will not reap."

We give out of a decision, a lifestyle we've intentionally adopted, not out of emotion. Our lives and decisions are principle centered, not emotion led. Adopt a lifestyle of consistent giving as a habit, and you will reap.

## KEEP SOWING IN DIFFICULT TIMES

If you're sowing and you don't see results for a long time, especially if you're going through a difficult time, one Scripture verse among many you can dwell on is Psalm 126:5: "They that sow in tears shall reap in joy" (KJV). Sowing in tears means continuing to sow when you're in a difficult-to-go-through, hard-to-bear season of your life, a crisis when you feel like giving up.

During the times when people don't see any way out of the circumstances around them, some people stop giving. They stop sowing and planting. They agree with the devil who is telling them sowing isn't working and God isn't going to come through for them. The worst time to stop giving is in tough times. That's the time to give very generously and keep our minds on the big picture of what God is doing that we don't yet see.

Different types of seeds grow and yield a harvest in different amounts of time. Different types of soil also affect the way seeds sprout and grow. For example, the black soil of Iowa, where I'm from, is much more fertile than the soil of a desert state. Some types of seeds that we sow into the spiritual realm take longer than others to grow and yield a harvest, as well. Our waiting time for a particular harvest may be longer than others!

For those who are faithful and continue to "sow in tears" during those stressful times, including those times that go on for years, Psalm 126:6 tells us they ". . . shall doubtless come again with rejoicing . . ." (NKJV) ". . . as they return with the harvest" (NLT)!

God will turn around our captivity of difficult times as he did when he returned the exiled Israelites to Jerusalem. (v. 1 NKJV, NLT.) They ". . . were filled with laughter . . ." and ". . . sang for joy. And the other nations said, 'What amazing things the Lord has done for them'" (vv. 1-2 NLT). And they said, "Yes, the Lord has done amazing things for us! What joy!" (v. 3 NLT).

Galatians 6:9 tells us, "And let us not grow weary while doing good, for in due season we shall reap if we do not lose heart." Do not lose heart. Keep sowing in difficult situations, looking at the big picture, and you will reap!

When we become consistent in sowing, we become vessels, channels, who God knows He can trust to use the finances He supplies us for the greatest benefit as we do our part by taking the steps He gives us to fulfill our calling. And although we already have God's favor as we follow Him, we can increase in favor!

"And Jesus increased in wisdom and stature, and in favor with God and men" (Luke 2:52). This verse shows us we can increase in favor; we can have different levels or dimensions of favor.

To increase in favor, check yourself to be sure you're following God's desires rather than men's. Some people are men pleasers instead of God pleasers. They put their boyfriend, girlfriend, husband, wife, kids, job, or career before God. If we want God's best, we put Him first, seek Him first, and He will not only give us favor with men, but He will increase His favor on our lives. Matthew 6:33 tells us, "But seek first the kingdom of God and His righteousness, and all these things shall be added to you." God wants the best for you. Do your part to allow Him to bring it to you.

Tithe and give offerings—and give your best. Give generously. Give money, kindness, and love. Be rich in good works by sharing through deeds and words in a lifestyle of giving. Let God open the windows of heaven and pour out blessing and favor on your life so that there won't be room to receive it. These are superabundant blessings, but we can still increase in favor!

Expect God's favor and blessings to increase and overflow in your life!

# 14

# GOD IS FOR YOUR SECURITY

## SAFETY

When God opens the windows of heaven and pours out great blessings in the form of favor on our lives, the blessing includes protection. The favor that God surrounds the righteous with, like a shield (Ps. 5:12), provides protection. When we act on the opportunities God's favor brings us, we are being shielded by God often without knowing it.

God wants us safe and protected in a very crazy and dangerous world. Our part in experiencing God's safety is to listen to His voice and do what He says as a priority. Following His directions will keep us in a place of safety. And He even warns us of danger!

*God wants us safe and protected in a very crazy and dangerous world.*

## GOD IS FOR YOU

Years ago, before all the extra security measures were in use, I was with five other pastors attending a leadership conference in Israel. We were at the airport in Tel Aviv, standing in line on the tarmac to board a plane to fly back to the U.S. Suddenly, sirens went off; military in jeeps swarmed in and jumped out carrying machine guns. The military grabbed the man in front of us and threw him to the ground. He had a backpack with a bomb in it, and he was about to board the plane with us to blow it up!

In St. Louis, Kim had sensed something was wrong. She had a prompting from God and told her friend, "I just got a warning. Pastor is in trouble. We need to pray." They and their prayer group started praying the Word in Psalm 91, the best chapter in the Bible on God's protection, and God moved in a mighty way to protect us!

Psalm 91:1 tells us, "He who dwells in the secret place of the Most High shall abide under the shadow of the Almighty." Another version words this verse as, "He who dwells in the shelter of the Most High will remain secure and rest in the shadow of the Almighty . . ." (AMP). There is protection, security, and rest under the shadow of the Almighty.

Verse 4 says, "He shall cover you with His feathers, and under His wings you shall take refuge . . ." (NKJV), "He will cover you and completely protect you with His pinions" (AMP). Under His wings is refuge. We are covered and completely protected.

We abide under God's protection when we live and dwell in the secret place. We make God our dwelling place (v. 9) by staying close to Him through fellowship, keeping Him first in our lives, and going to Him and His Word before arriving at any decision. We saw in a previous chapter, Jesus said to abide in Him. (John 15:4.) When we keep close to God and dwell in Him through abiding in Jesus, we can stay under His protection! And we can easily hear the voice of the Holy Spirit.

# GOD IS FOR YOUR SECURITY | SAFETY

## BE LED

Sometimes I went to John Osteen for advice on how to handle a particular situation. He usually answered my question, "What should I do?" with two words: "Be led." I wanted a more complete response! Then one day, I realized when we know God and His Word, abide in Jesus, and follow the voice of the Holy Spirit, the advice of "Be led" in every area is the greatest wisdom and counsel we can ever receive. The Holy Spirit guides and warns us. He may say, "Don't go there right now," "Don't take that flight—schedule this one instead," or "Don't go that way to work."

His protection can be as dramatic as it was in Tel Aviv or more subtle, but either way, He always wants to protect us. In Tel Aviv, I was in the place He wanted, as were the other pastors, and He raised up other people to pray for our protection.

We may be walking in obedience, and dangerous events happen, but God works in many ways to protect us. His voice and His favor in leading Kim and me in the right direction have kept us from wrong relationships that could have led us to destruction. Later we were so thankful we never engaged in them. Obeying His voice to act on opportunities through the favor He has given us has kept us from accidents we didn't even know at the time could have happened. He protects us from harm. When we are in God's will, we are in the safest place to be in a dangerous world because we are where God can easily protect us. Here's a good prayer: "God, protect me from anyone or anything that wasn't sent by You."

We want to put God and His Word first so that we don't open the door to living in fear and dread of what's going on in the world today. If we're not in faith, we're in fear, and faith is the atmosphere where God resides. If we're living in fear, it's difficult to hear God's voice and stay in the place of ultimate protection He wants for us.

# GOD IS FOR YOU

## STAY IN THE PEACE JESUS PROVIDES

We also can't hear God's voice when we're irritable, angry, upset, and in strife and contention because we feel hurt. We hear His voice and instructions when we live in the peace Jesus provides.

Many believers in Jesus don't understand and take seriously the reality of how important the truth in James 3:16 is to their lives: "For where envying and strife is, there is confusion and every evil work" (KJV). This means believers who quarrel, fight, stir up strife, are bitter, hold grudges, and generally live in unforgiveness are not walking in obedience to God's Word. They are opening up opportunities for the devil to use.

The enemy wants us to be so confused and distracted when dealing with problems in life that we can't hear God. God wants to do His part to protect us, but if we can't seek, hear, and follow Him, we're moving into a potentially unprotected and unsafe place with our finances and other areas. The devil has ploys, but God has plans. Our heavenly Father is merciful and still moves to help us, including when we get off course and make mistakes! But we want to guard against holding on to hurt that may allow "confusion" and "evil work" to overtake us in our lives. The devil wants to keep couples, families, businesses, and churches caught up in strife because he wants it to lead to their destruction. Strife causes division. The devil wants to destroy the effectiveness of the church.

In Matthew 24, beginning in verse 3, we read Jesus's description of the sign of His coming and the end of the age. He will come back ". . . on the clouds of heaven with power and great glory" (v. 30)! We are seeing the list of descriptions in Matthew 24 happening today. One of these is offense: "And then many will be offended, will betray one another, and will hate one another" (v. 10).

People have always been offended, but we are seeing offense to a greater degree today. In the end times, betrayal will follow offense and hurt, and people will turn on one another in anger and hatred.

A literal translation words verse 10, "and then shall many be stumbled . . ." (YLT). If believers are hurt through an offense and hang on to it, that hurt will cause them to stumble, trip, and fall into the devil's trap, ". . . the net of the trapper . . ." (Ps. 91:3 NASB).

They often stop attending church, serving the Lord, and following Jesus as their Savior. They will backslide away from God. Matthew 24:12 says, "And because lawlessness will abound, the love of many will grow cold." Their hearts may become cold because they aren't living in God's love, and they will be indifferent to Him, no longer experiencing the joy of serving Him and fulfilling their purpose. They will build up walls and stop trusting and believing in people. They won't finish their race for God. (1 Cor. 9:24; 2 Tim. 4:7; Phil. 3:14.) And this downward spiral starts with a hurt.

*Don't let emotion from a hurt direct the course of your life away from all God has for you!*

The conditions in the end times we're already seeing will become more and more extreme. In other words, things will get worse. This is one reason it is so important to understand that God is for you and know how to do your part. When you act on what you know and allow God to do His part, He will keep you safe and prosper you no matter what is happening around you. And you will continue being effective in your walk in Him. Learn how to handle offense and anger God's way to continue moving ahead toward overwhelming victory. Don't let emotion from a hurt direct the course of your life away from all God has for you!

Genesis 26:15-33 shows us Isaac's example of how he dealt with a serious offense when he was prospering in the land of famine. The Philistines wanted to rob Isaac of his prosperity by stopping up his wells. Instead of becoming angry and offended, Isaac moved ahead in the grace of God, knowing he was blessed according to the covenant, and God restored to him what the devil had stolen through the Philistines! The Philistines left the wells alone, and Isaac said, ". . . For now the Lord has made room for us, and we shall be fruitful in the land" (v. 22).

Instead of becoming offended and starting on a destructive path of retaliation, Isaac followed God's ways. And as a result, God blessed Isaac abundantly with restoration and peace with all the glory going to Him. (vv. 26-33.)

## HOLDING ON TO HURTS ROBS US

We've all been hurt, and I'm sorry for that, but we live in a hurting, broken world, and we'll all be hurt again. People may have a grudge over something someone did to them; live in bitterness, resentment, anger, and unforgiveness; or even lie awake at night rehearsing what happened to them. They have decided they aren't going to let go of the hurt, but holding on to it will rob them of receiving all God wants to give them.

*There are no advantages to holding on to hurts.*

There are no advantages to holding on to hurts. Anger will not help us live the good life God wants for us, the abundant life, God's best for us. Angry people, believers, often blame others, even God, for their troubles instead of concentrating on what He wants them to do. As a result, they miss God's blessings and reaching out to others to bless them.

Hebrews 12:15 warns of losing favor and blessing through harboring bitterness. "Look after each other so that none of you fails to receive the grace of God. Watch out that no poisonous root of bitterness grows up to trouble you, corrupting many" (NLT).

We know that hurt people hurt people, but hurt people also hurt. Because they're holding on to unforgiveness, they're living in the

## GOD IS FOR YOUR SECURITY | SAFETY

emotional misery that comes from hurt feelings. Unforgiveness takes away our happiness. Holding on to hurts can cause depression and harm our health. (Prov. 17:22.)

And if we don't let go of our hurts, we'll miss opportunities God has for us to tell people about His goodness and Jesus. We'll lose our witness. Once a cashier in a grocery store line who didn't go to our church told Kim and me, "You and your church are known all over for all the charity and good works that you do in our community." That's an example of our witness, to be like Christ. We want to ". . . overcome evil with good" (Rom. 12:21).

Many people don't understand how significant the difference is between the high price and penalty of holding on to what somebody did to them compared to the freedom that comes with release from the bondage of unforgiveness.

The people who hurt us may not deserve forgiveness; they may have been in the wrong; they may have been responsible for devastating loss in our lives. Yet it's too expensive for us to hold on to the hurt they caused.

Matthew 6:15 tells us, "But if you do not forgive men their trespasses, neither will your Father forgive your trespasses." I know that I serve a forgiving God and need Him to forgive me; I need God's forgiveness every day. How about you?

With God's help, we can let go of the hurts.

### HOW TO FORGIVE

We need to know how to respond so the hurt doesn't hold us hostage. How do we keep ourselves from becoming offended and angry? How do we eliminate the anguish, offense, scar, wound, and pain over an offense we already have? The answer is this: we forgive people.

How do we do that? Forgiveness in the Bible means to let a hurt go and let it drop. We forgive by letting the hurt drop. Let it go, let it drop, and get on with your life.

You may say, "Forgive? I don't know how to do that! I don't see how I can let those things go and drop. How in the world am I supposed to forgive people who have hurt me?" Forgive your enemies, nothing will annoy them more!

To let hurt go, we must start by being willing to let it go.

First, realize things will happen that will hurt and offend you. (Luke 17:1.) We live in a broken world.

The key is to know how to respond to the offense biblically. Being able to forgive isn't a matter of wishful thinking. Ephesians 4:32 shows us that when we're walking in God's love, we can forgive as He forgives! God wouldn't tell us to forgive without giving us the power to do it.

How does God forgive? When God forgives, He forgets. (Isa. 43:25.)

Some believers think, *I'll forgive them, but I'll never forget what they did to me!* That's living out of natural love. That's the best it can do. However, forgetting doesn't mean that if the other person's actions put you in danger, you should forget about the danger and stay in the situation. Instead of being ruled by anger or bitterness over the hurt, you should let God help you leave the resentment behind and move on to where He wants you.

When we confess our sins, God is faithful to forgive us. (1 John 1:9.) This is a fresh start. We don't deserve forgiveness or earn it. It's a gift. But the hard part is applying the same kind of forgiveness in our relationships. It doesn't matter what people did to us, how much they hurt us, or the negative results we experienced as a result, because God's love will enable us to forgive and forget and move forward in freedom with Him.

Second, recognize the hurt or offense is a trap, a "net," set by the enemy to trip us, get us to stumble and go off course, and keep us from finishing our race. Realize it isn't a person hurting you; it's the spirit behind the person. (Eph. 6:12 NLT.) To forgive is to set the prisoner free—and discover the prisoner was you.

The devil is behind it, and the Bible says to watch out for his attacks. (1 Pet. 5:8-9 NLT.) Our enemy isn't a person who hurt us, a political party, or other people in any category. We have one great enemy, the real one, the devil, our adversary. We need to stand fast in the victory Jesus gave us as joint heirs with Him (Rom. 8:16-17) over the devil (Col. 2:15) and not fall into his "net" as his victims.

Knowing it's the spirit behind the person we're dealing with helps us forgive the person. Hopefully, believers are influenced by the Holy Spirit rather than an evil spirit lying to us. First John 4:4 KJV that we looked at previously, ". . . greater is he that is in you, than he that is in the world," refers to the Holy Spirit and the devil and his evil spirits. The Holy Spirit in you is greater than the evil, demonic spirits in the world.

*Refuse to be offended. It is a choice.*

Third, refuse to be offended. It is a choice. Many times when someone hurts us, we need to communicate with that person about the hurt in a nonconfrontational way without throwing blame or displaying excessive emotion. Sometimes this will resolve the hard feelings. But in any case, we can drop a hurt and let it go, or we can hold on to it and be miserable with our hurt feelings, then turn around and hurt others, often those we love the most. When Kim and I fussed and fought in our early years, our kids picked up that strife and took it to school, then *they* got in trouble. Our trouble at home was contagious.

Resentment is too heavy a weight to have. (Prov. 27:3 NLT.) God doesn't want us to carry a heavy load of hurt. He wants us to unload our pain on Him by casting our burden on Him. If we find we're running to people more than God with and about our hurts, we have a closer relationship with people than God. God is the one who can help us most, and He is the one who will sustain us and work on our behalf.

Fourth, control your emotions. When you're working out in the gym and doing the exercises correctly and consistently, you're building as many little disciplines as you can into a big discipline. It's called the compound effect. Use this technique with your feelings. Keep making this choice over and over: refuse to be offended and ask the Holy Spirit to help you control your emotions—we can't do it on our own. Whenever we choose this, we apply the compound effect and build our character. God is interested in character, in us being Christlike, not in charisma. We believers are not of this world, just as Jesus was not. (John 17:16.) We live according to the ways of God's kingdom, not the ways of the world.

When we choose to take the high road and act like Christ, continuing to build our character, we're on our way to promotion into the next part of God's plan for us.

Fifth, renew your mind daily in God's Word. We are susceptible to enormous negativity through social media and the internet. It's crucial to dwell on less of the bad news and more of the good. Both unforgiveness and forgiveness start with a thought—unforgiveness with a negative thought and forgiveness with a positive thought. To recover quickly and bounce back from hurt, we need to renew our minds to the truth and counteract the negative with the positive from the Word. We gain strength from regularly renewing our minds in the Word to transform us.

Sixth, respond the right way—with God's love. First Peter 4:8 tells us, "Above all things have intense and unfailing love for one another, for love covers a multitude of sins [forgives and disregards the offenses of others]" (AMPC). This means we don't keep talking about a hurt and bringing it up. We don't post our pain on social media or keep reminding ourselves of it. Hurting people who hold on to hurts eventually hate. Hate stirs up trouble, but love forgives all offenses.

*"Who do I need to forgive?"*

The Bible contains a great deal of advice on relating to people and handling situations in life, including "... be quick to listen, slow to speak, and slow to get angry. Human anger does not produce the righteousness God desires" (James 1:19-20 NLT).

Remember the costs of unforgiveness. It blocks our fellowship with God. Then all of a sudden, we don't hear God's voice, and we're not in the place where we had been with God because of holding on to a hurt. We can't get a new revelation from the Word because it isn't alive to us. Unforgiveness blocks the answers to our prayers. If we want our prayers answered and God working in our lives, we can't afford to walk in unforgiveness. God wants to bless us and others through us.

Seventh, stop replaying the hurt. If you want to forgive someone or let the hurt drop, stop thinking about it! Let it go, and move forward.

Here's a powerful question to ask yourself every day: "Who do I need to forgive?"

God is for you and not against you. It is God's will for you to walk in health, prosperity, power, peace, purpose, and forgiveness. Decide to forgive.

## DON'T FALL FOR A TRAP IN ANY AREA

Besides the traps the devil sets when he can take advantage through strife, he sets other snares, but God is ready to protect us.

After Kim's mother passed on to heaven, Kim and I drove to the Iowa funeral. At four o'clock in the morning, in the pitch darkness, a man in a big truck pulling a trailer in the lane next to us started coming into our lane. I honked the horn, and we yelled and avoided a horrific collision. We praised the Lord for His protection. We could have been killed. That was a trap of the devil.

Angels are around us to protect us. (Ps. 34:7; Ps. 91:11.) Once when Kim was driving a horse trailer to another city, the trailer started going off the road. Another vehicle was coming, and she said it had to be angels protecting her because the trailer lifted and was put back on the road! Psalm 91:11-12 says, "For He shall give His angels charge over you, to keep you in all your ways. In their hands they shall bear you up, lest you dash your foot against a stone." Angels are with you everywhere you go.

The devil wants to take us out, but the Word tells us God will rescue us from every trap and protect us, even from a plague! (Ps. 91:3 NASB.) We can live according to verse 2 (NASB), which tells us God is our refuge and fortress. We can trust in Him to protect us! Believers have a restraining order against satan.

There are methods in the natural realm to protect our families and ourselves, such as with a security system. Still, we need to know where our absolute safety comes from, which is supernatural.

We have a legal right to access God's protection when we do our part to receive it. Let go of offense, and don't let the devil trap you by leading you into strife and unforgiveness. Live in obedience to God and His Word. Speak in line with the Word to build your faith and believe that what you're saying and confessing will happen. Obey, confess the Word, and believe He will do what He said He will do.

Abide in God and experience His supernatural supply in every area, including protection!

# A FINAL WORD OF ENCOURAGEMENT

## Let God Show You that He Is for You

The basis for believing God is for us is understanding how much He loves us.

People may start in their relationship with God believing that He loves them, but then something happens along the way to persuade them (erroneously) that He doesn't. That was what happened to me when my brother Rick died. There was a season I went through when I was angry with God and couldn't forgive Him. Why did God let my brother die?

I am still unable to answer that question directly, but I know this: God gently led me on a journey of showing me His goodness, which replaced the answer I had been seeking. As a result, I learned, understood, and believed the truth that God is for us. He is good and always looking for ways to work on our behalf when we let Him because He loves us. He never wavers from wanting good for us. He wants to help us succeed in every way to fulfill our potential and purpose and live a life immeasurably more abundant than we could imagine as we follow Him.

Many people reach that point of asking why God let a terrible thing happen. It was hard to walk through that time of Rick's death. And the lesson was hard for me to learn, one that we all need to learn. I had to get past the "Why?" and ask God, "What?" "God, what do You want me to learn from this? What do You want me to do now? What's next?" When I originally asked, "Why?", God responded in a way I wouldn't have anticipated. He brought me to a place of restoration and enthusiasm in moving forward with Him into the "What's next?" He had for me.

To firmly believe God loves us and is working for us, we need to pursue as a priority renewing our minds to the Scripture passages on love.

Transforming our thinking by renewing our minds doesn't happen overnight. It's a process. We need to be patient. We're not perfect, and, at times, we will fall back into old thought patterns of believing the lies the accuser is telling us. But we must take the thoughts into captivity, get back in the process, and stay there. The compound effect from rehearsing the Scriptures over and over about God's love for you will eventually transform you into a new person by changing the way you think!

We may be living in the most difficult days we've ever experienced. To get through and succeed, we need to be resilient. Resilience simply means having the ability to bounce back. It means not giving up and knowing how to depend on God for strength. Resilience is the ability to adapt, adjust, and be a student in the storm to stay on course. We need resilience if we're going to accomplish what God put us on this earth to do and finish our race. When we're resilient, we're tough, we make it through, rise up, and overcome.

It used to take Kim and me weeks to bounce back from some of the setbacks we were hit with. We learned that we could shorten that recovery time from weeks to days, a day, a few hours, then minutes. Let go of pride

# A FINAL WORD OF ENCOURAGEMENT

and blaming others so that you can hear what God is telling you. Don't be a victim—be a victor. Stop hurt from growing into bitterness. Forgive others, including anything you may be holding against God and yourself! Forgive, forget, and press forward to receive all God has for you.

Establish and live a daily routine of God-directed habits, including frequently meditating on the Word. Obey and serve where God directs. Focus on walking into the future He has for you.

Renew your mind daily to God's love for you. Move intentionally and forcefully ahead in that love, knowing God is for you, and fulfill your purpose with excellence in the way God planned!

# Author Contact

If you would like to contact David Blunt, find out more information, purchase books, or request him to speak, please contact:

David Blunt
900 Birdie Hills Rd.
Saint Peters, MO  63376
636.240.7775
www.cotr.org
pastordblunt@cotr.org

Follow David Blunt!
YouTube: @godisforyouexperience
Instagram: @davidmblunt